NOMINATING A PRESIDENT:
The Process and the Press

NOMINATING A PRESIDENT:
The Process and the Press

Edited by
John Foley
Dennis A. Britton
Eugene B. Everett, Jr.

Design by
Ken Bruns
Howard Anderson

PRAEGER
PRAEGER SPECIAL STUDIES • PRAEGER SCIENTIFIC

Library of Congress Cataloging in Publication Data
Main entry under title:

Nominating a President: The Process and the Press

1. Presidents—United States—Nominating—Addresses, essays, lectures.

I. Foley, John, 1923-
II. Britton, Dennis A., 1940-
II. Everett, Eugene B. Jr.

JK521.N65
324.5'4'0973
80-13824

ISBN 0-03-057858-2 (PB)
ISBN 0-03-057857-4

Published in cooperation
with the Los Angeles Times

Published in 1980 by Praeger Publishers
CBS Educational and Professional Publishing
A Division of CBS, Inc.
521 Fifth Avenue, New York, New York 10017 U.S.A.

0123456789 056 987654321

Printed in the United States of America

FOREWORD

Nominating a candidate to run for President of the United States used to be a relatively simple, straightforward process. It took only a few months, usually included a pleasant train trip and ended with much hoopla at the national party conventions. Like many organisms, however, the process has evolved into a complex, multifaceted creature. Today's candidates must be prepared to spend more than twice as much time seeking the nomination. They must appeal not only to party leaders, but also to voters. They must be prepared to compete in all manner of qualifying contests that are both part and prelude to primaries, caucuses and conventions. The candidates are at once beauty contestants, fund raisers, elucidators of profound policy, debators, accountants, economists, diplomats and persons of inexhaustible energy. The individuals in this race are no longer mere flesh and blood; they are electronic images—voices on the radio, heads on the television screen. The leisurely rail trip has given way to the frantic jet circus.

Now a candidate can be sold like a bar of soap—packaged, promoted, advertised and marketed to the American public in a way that has never before been possible. But along with the phenomenal change in the character of American politics came a similar change in the way Americans get their news. More journalists cover the political process than ever before, and this growing corps increasingly scrutinizes, analyzes and probes at the process and its participants. Covering the candidates has become a highly charged, competitive endeavor in which the Late Street Edition has been joined by the six o'clock news on television. Thus, any candidate's image, his perception by the public, is largely a blend of mass media images—the products of advertising and news reports in print and electronic media.

The Los Angeles Times and the Institute of Politics wanted to know what effect this evolution has had on nominating a President, in both the process and the press, and what modifications, if any, might be called for. We decided to bring together key political operatives and journalists who would be participating in and covering the 1980 presidential campaigns to share and develop ideas.

We picked a time—after the Iowa precinct caucuses and before the New Hampshire primary—and a setting—the Institute of Politics at Harvard's Kennedy School of Government—which we felt would help the participants openly discuss the inner workings, problems and peculiarities of the campaigns.

Selecting the participants proved most difficult. The roundtable format we had selected limited the participants to 25. The pool of possibilities, while limited, was still greater than that. In the process of developing the roundtable panels, many valuable persons were excluded. In addition, some of those who accepted an invitation to participate found due to unforeseen events they had to pull out at the last minute. One of the unfortunate side results of this was that we ended up with panels lacking minority or female representation.

Nevertheless, the balance and interplay between political operatives and journalists proved stimulating. The panelists were guided by moderators chosen for their experience in observing and participating in the nominating process but who were not directly active in the 1980 campaigns. Invited to hear the roundtables were special observers, including academicians, other journalists and political professionals.

This gathering—on the weekend of February 1-3, 1980—proved a stimulating break for those who had already spent months on the campaign trail and an invigorating stimulus for those just going out.

Appropriately we began on a chilly Friday night discussing the New Hampshire primary—whether it carries a disproportionate influence, whether it has been changed by new factors in the process, whether it is a *good* microcosm as opposed to an *accurate* microcosm. Later panels sorted out the differences between primaries and caucuses, attempted to get a handle on the effect of television, took a close look at press coverage of the issues and debated the effects of reforms and the desirability of further reforms.

These discussions offered a provocative and fascinating insight into the modern American electoral system and its nominating process. Far from a primer in politics, the roundtable discussions taken as a whole can be looked upon as a tour through a gigantic, complex machine, with a close look at some of the most interesting parts.

This book is basically a record of that tour, those roundtable discussions in Cambridge. While these conversations have been edited for clarity, the flavor of the spoken word hopefully is retained. At least that was the intention of the editors.

—JOHN FOLEY and DENNIS A. BRITTON

ACKNOWLEDGEMENTS

Were it not for the Los Angeles Times/Institute of Politics conference there would not be this book. And so in expressing acknowledgements, the editors must take special notice of those who made the conference a success.

Two who deserve unusual credit are Nancy Tew, administrative assistant to the editor of The Times, and George H. White, conference coordinator for the Institute. They spent long hours over a period of three months making major decisions that kept the conference on schedule and attending to the minutiae that added the fine touches to a well organized meeting.

Production of the book itself was under the supervision of Chong Lew of The Times' Promotion and Public Relations department, whose careful organization and attention to detail kept typesetting, printing and binding on schedule.

Our gratitude goes to members of the Institute's staff, Betsy Pleasants, administrative assistant; Karen Phillips, secretary to the director; Susan Elbow, financial and administrative assistant to the director, and Martin Linsky, consultant to the Institute on media programs. And for his wise counsel and steady hand, the editors are indebted to Nicholas T. Mitropoulos, assistant Institute director.

Among those from The Times who helped, special thanks go to Kathi Barr, secretary to the managing editor, for her day-to-day assistance; Sheila Daniel, who edited the manuscript and caught the subtlest of errors; Mary Pat Kelly of The Times Washington bureau, who helped speed the production of the book, and John Goldman of The Times New York bureau, who had an important role in the early conference planning. William Schneider, political consultant to The Times, gave invaluable help from the planning of the conference through the editing of the manuscript. George White also contributed to the editing and the organizing of the manuscript.

Ken Hively of The Times staff took the photograph for the back of the book, and Russell Arasmith, editorial art director of The Times, did the drawings of the moderators. The front cover photo is from Wide World.

CONTENTS

CONFERENCE PARTICIPANTS AND OBSERVERS

GRAHAM T. ALLISON
Dean
John F. Kennedy School
of Government

F. CHRISTOPHER ARTERTON
Associate Professor of
Political Science
Yale University

ALAN BARON
Editor
The Baron Report

RICHARD BERGHOLZ
Political Writer
Los Angeles Times

KENNETH A. BODE
Network News Correspondent
NBC News

WILLIAM BOYARSKY
City-County Bureau Chief
Los Angeles Times

DENNIS A. BRITTON
National Editor
Los Angeles Times

HALE CHAMPION
Senior Advisor to the President
Harvard University

OTIS CHANDLER
Publisher
Los Angeles Times

ADAM CLYMER
Reporter, Politics
The New York Times

ANTHONY DAY
Editor of the Editorial Pages
Los Angeles Times

JOHN D. DEARDOURFF
Chairman of the Board
Bailey, Deardourff & Associates

ROBERT J. DONOVAN
Senior-Fellow in Public and
International Affairs
Woodrow Wilson School
Princeton University

JAMES DOYLE
Washington Deputy Bureau Chief
Newsweek

MICHAEL S. DUKAKIS
Director of Inter-Governmental
Studies
John F. Kennedy School
of Government

JOHN FOLEY
Assistant Managing Editor
Los Angeles Times

DONALD FORST
Editor
Boston Herald American

JAMES GANNON
Editor
The Des Moines Register

JOHN J. GOLDMAN
New York Bureau Chief
Los Angeles Times

J. JOSEPH GRANDMAISON
Federal Co-Chairman
New England Regional
Commission

PETER D. HART
President
Peter D. Hart Research
Associates Inc.

ROBERT HEALY
Executive Editor
The Boston Globe

STEPHEN H. HESS
Senior Fellow
Brookings Institution

HAYNES JOHNSON
Columnist
The Washington Post

W. THOMAS JOHNSON
President
Los Angeles Times

DAVID R. JONES
National Editor
The New York Times

ROBERT J. KEEFE
President
The Keefe Company

DAVID A. KEENE
Political Director
George Bush for President

TIM KRAFT
National Campaign Manager
Carter/Mondale Presidential
Committee

I. A. LEWIS
Director, Los Angeles Times Poll
Los Angeles Times

MARTIN LINSKY
Media Programs Consultant
Institute of Politics

CHRISTOPHER LYDON
Anchorman of "10 O'Clock"
WGBH-TV

JESS MARLOW
Correspondent and Anchorman
KNBC News

JOHN P. MARTTILA
President
John Marttila & Associates, Inc.

WALTER R. MEARS
Vice President and Chief of Bureau
The Associated Press

NEWTON N. MINNOW
Partner
Sidley & Austin

NICHOLAS T. MITROPOULOS
Assistant Director and
Director of the Forum
Institute of Politics

JONATHAN MOORE
Director
Institute of Politics

JAMES M. NAUGHTON
Metropolitan Editor
The Philadelphia Inquirer

JACK NELSON
Washington Bureau Chief
Los Angeles Times

MARTIN F. NOLAN
Washington Bureau Chief
The Boston Globe

THOMAS QUINN
Campaign Manager
Brown for President

GEORGE E. REEDY
Professor of Journalism
Marquette University

ROBERT SCHEER
National Correspondent
Los Angeles Times

WILLIAM SCHNEIDER
Political Consultant,
Los Angeles Times
Visiting Fellow, Hoover
Institution Stanford University

ROBERT SHOGAN
Political Writer, Washington
Los Angeles Times

GEORGE SKELTON
Assistant Metropolitan Editor,
Politics
Los Angeles Times

WILLIAM J. SMALL
President
NBC News

HEDRICK SMITH
Washington Correspondent
The New York Times

FRANK STANTON
Former President
CBS, Inc.

RICHARD G. STEARNS
Chief of Delegate Selection
Kennedy for President Committee

DAVID A. STOCKMAN
United States Congressman
4th District, Michigan

ROBERT M. TEETER
President
Market Opinion Research

WILLIAM F. THOMAS
Executive Vice President and Editor
Los Angeles Times

JAMES TOEDPMAN
Executive Editor
Boston Herald American

CARL R. WAGNER
Director of Field Operations
Kennedy for President Committee

F. CLIFTON WHITE
President
F. Clifton White and Associates, Inc.

THEODORE W. WHITE
Journalist and Author

JAMES WOOTEN
News Producer
ABC News

NOMINATING A PRESIDENT:
The Process and the Press

ROUNDTABLE ONE

The New Hampshire Primary: Problems of Timing and Sequence

MODERATOR

Hale Champion is senior adviser to the president of Harvard University and to the dean of the John F. Kennedy School of Government. He has served in a variety of positions in government and education. He was director of finance in the administration of Governor Edmund G. Brown Sr. of California, vice president of finance at the universities of Minnesota and Harvard and from 1977 to 1979 undersecretary of the Department of Health, Education and Welfare. He has been a member of two presidential task forces. Mr. Champion attended the university of Michigan and Stanford and was a reporter for newspapers in California and Wisconsin.

PANELISTS

J. Joseph Grandmaison is federal co-chairman of the New England Regional Commission and has worked with the campaigns of Sen. George McGovern (D-S.D.), Sen. John A. Durkin (D-N.H.) and President Carter in 1976.

Robert J. Keefe is president of the Keefe Co. and an experienced political organizer who ran the 1976 presidential campaign of Sen. Henry M. Jackson (D-Wash.) in New England.

Walter R. Mears is vice president and chief of the Associated Press bureau in Washington.

Jack Nelson is Washington bureau chief of the Los Angeles Times.

Hedrick Smith is chief Washington correspondent of the New York Times.

Robert M. Teeter is president of Market Research, Inc. He has conducted polls for George Bush in 1980 and for others during the 1976 GOP presidential campaign.

ROUNDTABLE ONE

First Signals of Strength; Changing Campaign Styles; Interpreting the Results; A Choice of Battlegrounds; Picking a Winner; How the State Contests Differ; The Con and the Double Con; Press Coverage and the Polls; The Parochial Influence; The Numbers Game Again; A Homogenized America; Timing, Momentum and Psychology; Evaluating the Mix; Credibility and the Media; Summing Up.

First Signals of Strength

HALE CHAMPION: In order to put New Hampshire in its place without treading on it, I'm going to ask Bob Teeter to start. He's been doing some polling, and I think the question we might start with is, with the Iowa and Maine caucuses coming before and the Massachusetts and other primaries, and now primaries everywhere, is the New Hampshire primary what it used to be?

ROBERT M. TEETER: Well, it's still obviously very important, but I think the uniqueness in New Hampshire has been because of its order in the process, not because of anything inherent in New Hampshire itself. In terms of delegates, it's not particularly a large state, it's a small state for the type of politics there internally. And certainly now, compared to 15 or 20 years ago, it's a much smaller piece of the total. There were 12 or 13 primaries in 1952; now there are 37. So it's one of 37 instead of one of 12 or 13.

Secondly, there are a lot of things that come just before and just after it now, so it doesn't stand alone as much. We have the Iowa caucuses that do count that come right before it. There have been all kinds of off-year or prior-year events now—the Florida mini-conventions, Maine mini-straw votes, Iowa straw votes. So those are all first signals of strength, I think. But it's still at the same time the first primary. I think tradition if nothing else and its order make it important, and it is going to contribute a lot to the momentum, which is everything in the early stages of the primaries.

MR. CHAMPION: Let me turn to Joe Grandmaison and then let's just all join in it. Joe knows New Hampshire better than anybody else here: he lives there a good part of the time. And I'd like to have him comment not only on anything he has to say with respect to Bob's remarks, but also—is New Hampshire itself changing? Is the political complexion of the parties in the state changing at all? Is the population changing? Is New Hampshire not what it used to be because New Hampshire is different?

J. JOSEPH GRANDMAISON: There's no question that New Hampshire is changing in terms of the population, in terms of what makes up both membership in the party as well as the average voter. New Hampshire, I believe, is the fastest-growing state populationwise, something like east of the Mississippi. Rockingham County, New Hampshire, which is the southeastern tip, was a couple of years ago, I remember reading, the second fastest-growing county outside of Orange County, California. It has changed, the population has increased tremendously. New Hampshire does represent Americans, the voters, in terms of what their desires are. It's a changing population.

I think it's more important that a New Hampshire be first and that there be a state where the first major primary takes place, that is, a state that demands one-on-one campaigning of its candidates. A state that a candidate of modest resources can actually go into and state his case, whether it be door to door, whether it be with coffee klatches throughout that state.

If there had not been a New Hampshire in 1972, there would have been no George McGovern. And I'd suggest to you if there wasn't a New Hampshire—there probably wouldn't be a George Bush in 1980, because here is a state where a candidate, such as in Iowa, can go in and actually meet voters without having a ton of money behind him.

ROBERT J. KEEFE: If there hadn't been a New Hampshire and George McGovern, there might not have been a Richard Nixon. (Laughter)

MR. CHAMPION: I think it was very clear he was there.

MR. KEEFE: New Hampshire was never important because it was there. It was important because of when it was.

MR. GRANDMAISON: You mean first.

MR. KEEFE: First. The most important primary is always the next one. New Hampshire was the next one for the longest period since it was first. Simple as that.

JACK NELSON: Can a case be made, though, that New Hampshire this time may be just as important as before?

MR. KEEFE: No.

MR. NELSON: It can be.

MR. KEEFE: Not first, Jack.

MR. NELSON: Nevertheless, you have Bush coming out first in the Iowa caucuses. Then you have Jimmy Carter.

MR. KEEFE: Why?

MR. NELSON: I'll say why. If now Carter and Bush both win or happen to win in New Hampshire, it becomes, I think, extremely important.

MR. KEEFE: Only because they won in Iowa.

MR. NELSON: That's right. But it also makes it extremely important now.

MR. KEEFE: The *next* primary is the most important one. Right now New Hampshire is next.

MR. NELSON: Sen. Edward M. Kennedy said if he didn't make it—he's changed his mind since then—but he said if he didn't make it in New Hampshire, didn't make it in Maine, he would not be a viable candidate. It seems to me that makes New Hampshire an extremely crucial state.

MR. KEEFE: On June 1 (two days before the California primary), the most important primary will be California because it's the next.

MR. GRANDMAISON: That presumes he will be a candidate until June 1.

WALTER R. MEARS: That's the point we ought to address. The New Hampshire primary is a winnowing process. It's most important in saying who goes on and who doesn't, as are all the early primaries. Later on you get into the point where you slug it out for delegates. But the key in the first two months, six weeks, is who is going to be there when you get to California, who is going to be there for Pennyslvania (April 22) for that matter.

MR. CHAMPION: New Hampshire doesn't really determine that yet, except maybe to the extent that some of you think or say that it does.

HEDRICK SMITH: I'd like to go back to what Jack Nelson said. I disagree. I find it interesting we are starting to talk about New Hampshire.

MR. NELSON: Disagree with me?

MR. SMITH: Yes, with you. In a way we ought to be talking about Iowa because it did this year what New Hampshire traditionally does, which is to start that winnowing process and set up what happens next. Your comment about what Sen. Kennedy said would not have been made had he done better in Iowa or if there had been no Iowa.

MR. MEARS: His first comment was that the straw vote in Florida wasn't real and that the first real test was Iowa. As Bob Keefe said, the next primary, the next test is always the key one. The question is, how long can you keep saying that? At the point that you can no longer say that, you are no longer a candidate; you are winnowed. (Laughter)

MR. SMITH: The point is in Iowa you get to the start of the actual process of selecting delegates. It's not the delegates that come down. It's a sense there's a starting gun. With Florida in the straw polls, there isn't. There's a starting gun that used to begin in New Hampshire because you were going for a delegate.

MR. MEARS: Delegates don't really count. The Carter people at that point are already saying that no matter what happens in New Hampshire, they will have more delegates on February 26 because Minnesota will select 75 delegates to New Hampshire's 19.

MR. TEETER: The importance of where the momentum really starts for somebody was always New Hampshire before now. That was the first time that anybody could start going anywhere. And now it's either Iowa or it's the Florida mini-conventions or the Maine straw vote or four or five other things, and one that counts, Iowa, just happened before New Hampshire. That's at least started. It used to be that New Hampshire was first and did what Iowa did and maybe Florida did what New Hampshire does now as the second step in the process. I think the whole thing that makes it unique is simply the order.

Changing Campaign Styles

MR. MEARS: One thing that I think has changed, unfortunately, is the notion of one-on-one campaigning, of a place where candidates actually meet people. I think that's past us in New Hampshire and everywhere else. The first New Hampshire primary I covered was in 1964, and you actually went with guys who had two or three people around them and met people. Even four years later that had changed. I remember being in a sporting goods store with George Romney and three television crews and 15 reporters.

MR. KEEFE: Lyndon Johnson didn't do that in 1964.

MR. MEARS: Any candidate who goes in there and is a viable candidate at the point he gets there is surrounded by such a crowd of us that you no longer have the one-on-one.

MR. GRANDMAISON: The good campaign tends to make up for that in terms of the type of events, how they are structured. No question Sen. Kennedy is at a severe disadvantage when they have a motorcade of 22 cars whisking through holding up traffic.

MR. MEARS: He wasn't going around by himself.

MR. TEETER: A year ago he was.

MR. GRANDMAISON: So did Jimmy Carter.

MR. SMITH: One-on-one this year is on the telephone. It's Jimmy Carter talking to people. That is the retail politics of 1980. It's a very different style.

MR. CHAMPION: Let me come back and raise another kind of fundamental question. The premise is that the first primary ought to be a place where politics is one-on-one instead of the way politics is in the major industrial states. Are the complexions of those places sufficiently representative of the country to have them be good places to do the winnowing? And let's talk about New Hampshire in those terms.

MR. SMITH: One of the most striking things to me as a newcomer to this whole process is that both New Hampshire and Iowa are states where people take politics terribly seriously. They get engaged, they get involved, they respond. There are activist traditions which are remarkable, and it seems to me that's one of the things that makes them good microcosms. They aren't accurate microcosms, either one of them, on the contrary. You don't have many minorities in either one of them, you don't have major industrial areas. You can argue the primary process, if it started with Iowa and New Hampshire or New Hampshire and Iowa, then very quickly it ought to move to Illinois or Pennsylvania or California or New York or some other kind of state, or a southern state, but it moves too slowly to those larger states.

MR. MEARS: It moves very rapidly to Massachusetts, where Sen. Henry M. Jackson last time won after not entering New Hampshire and the win didn't do him a bit of good.

MR. TEETER: I noticed that. (Laughter) Wherever you start, if you start in California, which is as big as you can start in, the candidates would have two years to work it. They would be in Stockton at the morning lineup to get the jobs—Mexicans coming out to get the jobs—they would be down there shaking hands with them. They would be.

MR. CHAMPION: Look, you're back in a place where I did a lot of campaigning. There are 20 million people. You don't shake their hands. You don't have somebody saying, I'm sorry, I can't vote for him, I never met him. That doesn't happen.

MR. KEEFE: They (the candidates) would be doing a very different thing in California.

MR. TEETER: There very clearly are states where people expect to see the candidate because of the tradition of politics—some of those are big states, some of them medium and some small—New Hampshire and Iowa. A big such state is Michigan, simply because of G. Mennen (Soapy) Williams (Michigan's highly accessible governor from 1949 to 1961).

MR. KEEFE: They don't expect presidential candidates, do they?

MR. TEETER: I think they do in the primary. You go to a state like Pennsylvania, there's no expectation at all. I don't think in California people expect to actually see the candidates. That's a tradition unique to each state, and I'm not sure it has that much to do with the size of it.

Curiously, we did a poll in New Hampshire of Republican primary voters about a month apart last fall in November and we did one nationally. When you look at the Republicans in New Hampshire compared to Republicans nationally, there are very, very few differences. Their primary voters are not very different from Republican primary voters in Maine.

MR. CHAMPION: Is that true of the Democrats as well?

MR. KEEFE: How many states can't you say that about since television came in and homogenized America?

MR. TEETER: Primarily the southern states.

MR. KEEFE: Among Republicans.

MR. NELSON: You only say that among Republicans.

MR. TEETER: That's right.

MR. NELSON: What about Democrats? They are not typical at all. (Laughter)

MR. TEETER: Democrats in New Hampshire are more different than Democrats are nationally because you don't have large concentrations of blacks, you don't have big industrial cities, large concentrations of union members, which you do in a lot of other Democratic primaries.

MR. MEARS: I think Bob Teeter's point on this question of the kind of campaigning you do and the kind of tradition of the state is a very valid one. That is, no matter what the state—New York State, New York City—if that started it, and if a George Bush or a Jimmy Carter or whoever had to go in there when he couldn't draw a crowd . . . . Carter used to talk about having a news conference in Philadelphia one time and nobody came. If you can draw a thousand people, you deal with a thousand people. If the only way you can campaign is to go door-to-door, you go door-to-door and you're one-on-one, and it doesn't make any difference if it's New Hampshire or Florida or California, whatever. It's the order that determines that.

Interpreting The Results

MR. GRANDMAISON: I don't think anybody can question the importance of New Hampshire, because it's always been first. Obviously that's the key ingredient. I wanted to ask Bob in the campaign he ran in 1976, were you urging your candidate to go into New Hampshire to state his case?

MR. KEEFE: Not really, because Scoop Jackson had a peculiar problem in that the media, the guys on the other side of the table (the press), posed the situation where he was a loser and we couldn't start by losing. So we had to start by winning and you cannot lose in two ways. You can either win or not enter and not entering was sure better than losing. You had a better shot of winning Massachusetts.

MR. NELSON: Fact is, he's not a very good one-on-one campaigner.

MR. KEEFE: He wasn't spending time at it.

MR. SMITH: Did you really win in the long run? Because by not entering you never really got started. I mean, although you won in Massachusetts, you never caught up with the race. Can't you argue that the failure to enter in New Hampshire was—

MR. KEEFE: If we had started and lost we would have been over then, instead of three weeks later.

MR. SMITH: Save a lot of effort.

MR. KEEFE: True. April 27 we got out. Had we entered in New Hampshire we might have ended on March 2.

MR. GRANDMAISON: I disagree. I happen to think in 1972 and 1974 Scoop Jackson could have done exceptionally well, if not won, New Hampshire's primaries. We discussed that both years.

MR. CHAMPION: I think we have got a good chance here to start thinking in terms of these kinds of political strategies and political choices, in terms not only of New Hampshire, but of the way in which the press treats New Hampshire and why it has used New Hampshire as it has; not just the winnowing, the fundamental question of is it what happened there—the numerical results—or is it the interpretation? How do you decide which people are out after New Hampshire? How do you decide who has momentum and what the momentum is? Let's look at New Hampshire last time and then talk about it in those terms.

MR. MEARS: Sen. Jackson kept going well into the spring in the last campaign. He finally got out because of money. That's what knocks the field down. The money doesn't come. You can say that it's what we write that determines whether they get the money.

MR. NELSON: Matter of fact, Rep. Morris K. Udall of Arizona went much longer than Jackson did and again he never finished first. It wasn't the press that kept him from finishing first. He frankly ran out of funds.

MR. MEARS: As long as you got money in the bank you keep going.

A Choice of Battlegrounds

MR. SMITH: I think there's something more fundamental. I think of New Hampshire as something of a prototype—this year I would say Iowa. I think it was very significant that Sen. Kennedy did say before the Florida caucuses that Iowa was the first test. He set that battleground; it was his quote in terms of Carter and Kennedy this year. That was set by Sen. Kennedy openly.

But it's also interesting that President Carter sent Bill Romjue out to Iowa in April, long before any reporters had been thinking very much about it. He was already figuring that Iowa was going to be a battleground. Similarly, so did George Bush on the Republican side. I don't think, in fact, that we set the battlegrounds. I think the candidates set the battlegrounds.

MR. CHAMPION: Except they read you in 1976 on the Carter thing, particularly when the Republicans saw that was where you went from one percent —from the asterisk—to something.

MR. NELSON: This was not new, though, that a candidate got momentum in the Iowa caucus. Carter got that in 1976 in the same way.

MR. MEARS: By losing.

MR. NELSON: Nevertheless, he got momentum by doing much better than anybody thought he would do. Matter of fact, I still remember him sitting in the Washington Bureau of the L.A. Times when everybody still said Jimmy Who? and laying out his whole battle plan and saying, "I'm going to do well in Iowa," and everybody laughing at him.

MR. TEETER: What made Iowa important this year—not because Kennedy said it would be the battleground—was simply the order, that it came first, it was the opening gun. It's because nobody had done well; not Sen. Jackson or anybody else who tried to pick and choose their way through the primaries.

People who have done well are those who said this is the order, these are the cards we have been dealt. They start out with the first one and run hard to finish first.

MR. MEARS: That is in the last two campaigns, since the McGovern rules took effect.

MR. TEETER: That's right, since we have had 30 primaries or 35 instead of 15.

MR. MEARS: You did pick and choose before that. What did John Kennedy run, six primaries?

MR. TEETER: That's right. There were only half as many primaries then.

MR. MEARS: There has been a very basic change in the process. Primaries were where you proved you had appeal in this part of the country and New Hampshire and the Midwest and California. Now it's an entirely different process.

MR. TEETER: That's important—the fact since 1972 it has been different.

MR. CHAMPION: Let me ask, in reporting on New Hampshire, do you take the view that it is necessary to sort of say what it is and what it is not as well? We have had several years now of discussion of this order, of sequence, and a lot of people think it's unfair, they will say it's unfair to the country. Here we have a couple of small states, politically active one-on-one campaigning. That isn't the way, predominantly, presidential candidates are chosen. Do you think the press succeeds in keeping these in perspective, or does it in matter of fact dry up money, change the pattern of the campaign? The strategists feel that it is the press treatment. Do they feel the press could do a better job in discounting, if indeed these things should be discounted?

MR. MEARS: How would we discount a contest if the candidates choose to make a major contest, as witness Florida goings-on this year?

MR. KEEFE: Look at the record. In Iowa what was Bush's percentage versus Reagan's?

MR. MEARS: 31-29.

MR. KEEFE: On election night it was reported as a seven-point win—which made him look like a world-beater.

MR. SMITH: Couldn't have been, because the returns didn't get to that figure until 4 or 5 a.m.

MR. KEEFE: Why report it until 4 or 5 a.m?

MR. MEARS: You mean ignore it.

MR. KEEFE: Report it accurately. There are two phenomena.

MR. NELSON: Reports were as of that time.

MR. KEEFE: I understand.

MR. MEARS: When they quit counting on election night they had 76 percent of the precincts counted.

MR. KEEFE: I remember John Sears saying, wait until western Iowa comes in. Everybody was discounting the fact that western Iowa was going to come in and change the results. It changed them dramatically from a seven-point race to a point and a half race.

MR. SMITH: I take issue. Everybody didn't ignore western Iowa. Some papers indicated that western Iowa and some of the Reagan areas—

MR. KEEFE: Nobody said it was a real close race.

MR. GRANDMAISON: It doesn't make much difference—seven or a point and a half, George Bush won and deserved to have it reported.

Picking a Winner

MR. TEETER: That points to another problem with press coverage. That is being able to set up a false number and say if somebody doesn't get 30 percent they lose or if they get 40 percent they win. Whoever comes in first wins. It doesn't matter whether it's seven points or a point and a half. In any one of these primaries, I don't see how you can lose and come in first and I don't see how you can win and not come in first. It seems to me, in winner-take-all politics, which is what we have in this country, you either win or don't win it.

MR. KEEFE: Carter was set up in Iowa. Had he won by eight points he would have lost.

MR. TEETER: I agree with that. That's a fault.

MR. MEARS: I don't agree with that. I think that the Carter people had managed, despite all that was written about the polls, to set it up as a "somebody wins, somebody loses" race. The Reagan people came in and said we are going to win. John Sears was confident they were going to win. They lost.

MR. SMITH: I think your point is valid. If Reagan had won 31-29 over Bush, the winner in the Republican race would have been Bush. Bush would have been seen as the winner psychologically even had he lost by two points.

MR. CHAMPION: Seen by whom?

MR. SMITH: I think he would have been seen by political professionals, people sitting across the table from us and not just us in the press. I think that's exactly where we get an awful lot of the assessment.

MR. CHAMPION: A lot of that assessment is self-serving. How do you sort that out?

MR. SMITH: You know Bob Teeter is a good guy. (Laughter)

How the State Contests Differ

MR. TEETER: Let us assume Iowa is important because it was first, New Hampshire is important because it's second and it's the first primary. It seems to me after that is when you really do get into substantial differences. The press is going to cover Florida, I suspect, to a much greater degree than it may cover Alabama or Georgia or South Carolina. There are states that are picked out as we go along. I'm never been quite sure whether that's because of tradition or the hotels are a little nicer there or whether the food is better or whether it's geography or simply size of the state. It clearly is true, I think, as we get through, Florida already has and probably will get more attention than Alabama or South Carolina.

MR. MEARS: Compare the states.

MR. TEETER: Is it size?

MR. MEARS: Florida is a much more cosmopolitan state. There's much more of a blend there than in Alabama.

MR. TEETER: What you're saying is size is important.

MR. MEARS: I think size and makeup are important.

MR. KEEFE: Tell me why the coverage in Wisconsin on April 6, 1976, was greater than in New York on April 6, 1976, if size is important to you, cosmopolitan makeup, etc.

MR. MEARS: The Wisconsin primary in 1976 became important because of what happened when Udall thought he had won and it turned out he hadn't. That was something different. Also the New York primary—one problem with New York primary: it was still under that system where you ran anonymously and said I might be for Jackson but I'll tell you several months from now.

MR. KEEFE: No.

MR. MEARS: Yes. That was an awful system.

MR. SMITH: It has a great deal to do with which candidates pick certain states as battlegrounds, not size. If there is a real head-to-head between John Connally and Ronald Reagan in South Carolina—and that may mean the end of the Connally candidacy if he doesn't carry it off—that will get a lot more coverage than if both of them put in a mediocre effort there. I think George Bush is laying a surprise in Alabama. You may suddenly find there's a lot more coverage going toward Alabama than Florida if it looks as though it's a pretty clear-cut expected result.

MR. CHAMPION: John Connally has postered South Carolina. You have all been told.

MR. SMITH: I believe, even if we hadn't had the results we had in Iowa, that Maine would have been covered by some people wisely because I believe the Carter forces were lying in ambush for Teddy Kennedy long before Iowa took place. Anybody following the political process learned that and got themselves ready. I think what's happening is the sharp reporters are finding out where one politican and another is trying to make a move and seeing whether or not it worked.

MR. CHAMPION: Is there a question of whether the press might do this better by treating this whole thing as an historical process in which everything is in one period after another—having an election and not maybe second-guessing what the political professionals are asking you to do, not taking it as seriously?

MR. MEARS: Why do we not take it seriously? It's the process of electing a president.

MR. CHAMPION: I know. There are 50 states out there: 37 of them now have primaries, and yet there is vast portent written into what happens in Iowa and Maine, and it may in fact be portentous. There's not an argument about that. But the question is: You have got all of these other expressions to come, and yet you're going to say these people aren't going to be in it by the time you get to the industrial states.

MR. NELSON: The fact is, some people may not be in it. For example, Kennedy is really throwing all his resources into New England right now. If he does not do well in New England, how is he going to be in it after that? In fact he closed down his operations in Illinois. He doesn't have any operations going in the Southern primaries. He literally will be out of it.

MR. MEARS: Your question suggests an expansion on the notion that Bob Keefe offered a little while ago. That was that somehow we should not have reported that when the Republicans were through counting votes on the night of their caucuses in Iowa, Bush was six or seven points ahead. We should have waited until they were all in. We could wait until late May and then say, hey, they had all these primaries and guess what happened. (Laughter)

MR. CHAMPION: The question is, can you find some way to put it in the context of the whole process? Say, look, nobody wants people to not report anything, and what's factual is what you say about it.

The Con and the Double Con

MR. GRANDMAISON: Let me ask Bob Keefe a question. Is it the interpreting of the results that bothers you or is it the reporting of the results? Because I think when you get into the numbers game as to whether it requires one more vote over the other guy to have defeated him for nomination, to have won that primary, that is a matter of numbers. That's why every campaign employs experts at massaging the press so they can get their level of expectations as low as possible. Don't you think in order to report a primary situation with a half a dozen candidates or something in it, that the press has an obligation to do some intelligent interpreting of what candidacy is put into that race, or just give hard knocks?

MR. KEEFE: It is not unreal to ask the press to interpret what the politicians are trying to do and then judge them by what they are trying to do as opposed to how they do it. Okay. I believe that is an honest evaluation. They don't do it particularly well in my opinion because they believe us when we tell them things.

MR. GRANDMAISON: They know when we are conning them. Isn't that true? When Rick Smith calls and asks what's happening in New Hampshire—and I tell him all about these marvelous rallies, Carter rallies, so forth—he knows I'm conning him. (Laughter)

MR. CHAMPION: This game can get very complicated, conning and double conning and reconning.

MR. KEEFE: That's what the presidential race is.

Press Coverage and the Polls

MR. CHAMPION: I understand. Let's see if we can bring the discussion back to the New Hampshire primary. I'd like to get the sense from both sides of the table, what does New Hampshire mean this year? Is it in fact a place where the Democratic thing can be decided? Is it in fact a place where you confirm George Bush as a front-runner if he beats Reagan? What are the things that you can say about New Hampshire this year, and then are those things that really serve the process?

MR. SMITH: There's a missing party here, and the missing parties are not only the voters but the fund givers. One of the most striking things that happens after any set of results is either you get a lot more volunteers and a lot more money or you get a lot less money and a lot less volunteers. The network news could run the Iowa or New Hampshire results at the end of the 30 minutes instead of at the beginning of the 30 minutes, it could give it two minutes' time instead of 10 minutes' time. We could run it at the middle or the bottom of the front page instead of the top, but I bet you dollars to doughnuts that, regardless of how we played it, they would find out and they would go with whoever was winning or doing better than they thought—not only better than we think, but than they thought.

MR. CHAMPION: Does it play against something else, Bob, and maybe it would help if you commented on this, that it then plays into the polls nationally?

MR. TEETER: It does.

MR. CHAMPION: The people who give the money are going to see that. Do they work off the polls or something else?

MR. SMITH: I'm delighted you asked that question, because before we had much chance to interpret the results in Iowa, ABC, I believe, and Lou Harris took a poll, right away, within 24 hours, and George Bush had suddenly gone from that asterisk three percent to 29 percent, even with Ronald Reagan, as a result of the Iowa results. Those were, you know, fairly undiluted results, even if you allow for the four percent or three percent or seven percent. This was just raw fact hitting the public.

MR. TEETER: Iowa was important because it was first, New Hampshire is important because it's second. You can substitute Texas, South Dakota, Florida. If they happen to be in that order, they are going to have a lot to do with momentum. Whoever won, they will get more volunteers and money and go up in the polls. Those are simply facts.

As long as you're going to have 36 events, one of them has to be first and another has got to be second and another has got to be third and somebody has got to be last, unless you have some kind of a one-day national primary. The fact is that New Hampshire will be important, but the reason it will be important is because it's second.

MR. MEARS: The first in which the Kennedys pick a fight. In 1976 nobody paid any attention to the Republican outcome in Iowa, which was a virtual tie between Ford and Reagan.

MR. TEETER: But Iowa is the first real place, the starting gun. That's the first place where any delegates are chosen.

MR. MEARS: Candidates in 1984 will not be able to afford not to go there.

MR. KEEFE: There was a big difference again in 1976 and 1980 in the attention paid to Iowa by your side (the press) and this side of the table.

MR. MEARS: The attention begins on your side of the table. If they (the candidates) don't go there, there's no fight.

The Parochial Influence

MR. KEEFE: New Hampshire is going to be more important in the Democratic primary process this year, simply because it's next door to Massachusetts, Sen. Kennedy's home, than it would be if the second primary were someplace else or if Sen. Kennedy were from Indiana.

MR. CHAMPION: That's an important general question. Is there a parochial influence? Should we be expecting people to do better in their own territory? Or is this disappearing from the scene?

MR. SMITH: I happened to spend some time in New Hampshire this past week. They are talking about energy, Iran, Afghanistan. They are talking about the character and the style of a leader and how he would handle the presidency, either how Carter is doing it now or how Sen. Kennedy would do it or a shortfall of their expectations of him in the way he ran his campaign. And the fact that he's from next door seems to count this year now for much less than people would have thought six weeks ago.

MR. KEEFE: The New Hampshire/Massachusetts mix is more peculiar. I would guess something on the order of 25 percent to 30 percent of the people who can vote this year in New Hampshire have voted in Massachusetts when Sen. Kennedy was running.

MR. SMITH: What's interesting is a striking percentage of the people who moved from Massachusetts into New Hampshire have gone from being registered Democrats to being Independents.

MR. CHAMPION: They moved because of lower taxes.

MR. GRANDMAISON: That's exactly the point. Of course the press has to say if it's a neighboring state you expect him to get a larger percentage of the vote. Of course your ethnic ancestry or your religion when it's the same as the majority of the citizens that are going to vote in the Democratic primary, of course, that has to be taken into account. The problem for Sen. Kennedy is the fact all of those people who moved up from Massachusetts to New Hampshire moved for one reason —that's because of taxes. And unfortunately what he has to do somehow is say yes, I'm from Massachusetts, but I also have to disassociate myself with the reasons you physically moved from Massachusetts to New Hampshire, which is indeed high spending and high cost of government.

MR. MEARS: What happened so far is removed of the geographic handicap, say, that Muskie faced. He had to do this well. At this point a great many people feel Kennedy is likely to lose New Hampshire.

MR. TEETER: Take the Muskie example. Muskie was from a neighboring state to New Hampshire in 1972. We polled early in New Hampshire; Muskie didn't have any particular support any more than he had in Ohio, Illinois or Wisconsin. There are two things that make New Hampshire unique: A lot of people who are formerly Massachusetts people move into the media market; a large share of the prime media market in New Hampshire does come from Massachusetts, where Sen. Kennedy is from. I think that is what makes the difference, not that there happens to be a common border between the two states.

MR. CHAMPION: Didn't Rick Smith bring up a point that, in terms of the sailence of some of these things, it depends on what the overriding issues are. When you have Iran and Afghanistan and inflation and energy, things about which people get very concerned and to which they pay a lot of attention, then some of these other things (such as the candidate's home territory) tend to sink in the scale. They end up seventh or eighth, whereas if you didn't have those kinds of things they might be more important.

MR. KEEFE: You're absolutely correct. But they are not sinking in the interpretation of the New Hampshire primary in 1980. The question is, for 70 percent New Hampshire will be home for Kennedy, just as Alabama and Georgia will be home for the President the following week.

MR. CHAMPION: Are you saying that because you think that's the way the newspapers will read it or because that's the way everybody will see it?

MR. KEEFE: That's the way I read the newspapers.

The Numbers Game Again

MR. TEETER: Also, some things about Sen. Kennedy doing well whether he wins or loses. That's still a question. He can win New Hampshire by five votes and win it or lose it by five votes and lose it.

MR. CHAMPION: What does that mean? How much does he win and how much does he lose?

MR. TEETER: I think if he wins it, he won it.

MR. NELSON: I don't agree on that. If he loses New Hampshire or wins New Hampshire by a very close margin, in effect he does lose.

MR. TEETER: If he wins, he wins. He gets more than President Carter.

MR. NELSON: I happen to disagree with you. I think it's close. If it's very close, he's going to get a very small margin in the delegate count as well. It would be a big setback to him for it to be very close.

MR. GRANDMAISON: You're saying Kennedy can't get any pluses out of winning in New Hampshire unless it's a sizable victory, but Carter could score a knockout in New Hampshire.

MR. TEETER: Who decides what is substantial? Isn't that simply the press, the way they write it, whether 55 percent is substantial or 60? Is 53 substantial or 60?

MR. SMITH: If Ted Kennedy wins by a tenth of a percent, two votes in New Hampshire, it's a real victory.

MR. MEARS: If he wins, he gets a new wind.

MR. NELSON: If he wins, he wins by that very narrow margin, he gets very few delegate votes at the convention.

MR. MEARS: But there are 19 delegates. (Laughter)

MR. NELSON: Nevertheless, maybe only one delegate vote more than Carter. Then you go into the Southern primaries. I think he will lose campaign funds if he loses.

MR. KEEFE: All this is following the fact that we discussed earlier. It was important because he was so far ahead in New Hampshire earlier and wasn't that far ahead in Florida.

MR. MEARS: No, all I was saying was that I don't think the circumstances are those that Muskie faced. Bob Keefe was asking how you set these targets, who decides. They way the targets get set is that we talk to you guys (campaigners). And some of you are not smart enough not to tell us what you think is going to happen. So a Meldrim Thomson says, as Reagan's 1976 New Hampshire chairman, we are going to win with two-thirds of the vote. John Sears goes and seeks him out and tries to cut him up and can't—he keeps saying it. And Reagan loses with 49.6 percent of the vote, I think. Or Muskie's campaign manager says, I'll kill myself if we don't get 50 percent, so they don't.

MR. CHAMPION: Are we talking about a very inside game between the press and people who manage the political process? Is that a right way to have it? Shouldn't you have some other sources of judgment? How much do you have to play to the way the press sets the strategy and momentum? Are you victims or conspirators?

MR. TEETER: Both.

MR. CHAMPION: You both play the game.

MR. TEETER: That's right. A large part of the strategy and the way you go at a campaign and plan it has something to do with the way the press sets the stage for you and the way they are going to interpret what you do. But at the same time you are victims, you have to deal with what it is they write, and obviously everybody early on tries to play the game of poor-mouthing your own chances and saying we are only going to get 30 percent, when they really think they're going to get 40 and say it was a great win.

MR. MEARS: It changed since Muskie. Muskie's experience in 1972 drastically changed what campaign managers were likely to do. There was a time when they would love to run around and say, boy, we are going to wipe them out, because the theory was it turned on all your volunteers and brought out money. There it became evident it was risky to do. The game is: If I'm going to get three percent of the vote, I'm delighted. Bush's victory was a great boon to John Connally's campaign.

MR. GRANDMAISON: Or else you go in and take a poll to prove indeed you are expanding your base in blue collar communities and therefore it really was a victory. We secured the Jewish vote or whatever. Isn't that what you do in order to divert the attention from the fact you didn't get more votes than the other guy?

MR. SMITH: The marvelous thing is human fraility. Sure, that's what candidates and campaign managers, if they had it locked up drum tight, would like to do. But there's always somebody like Meldrim Thompson, or Muskie's manager. Things percolate down; if they don't say it directly to us, they say it to somebody who is supposedly neutral. You begin to find out what peoples' expectations are.

MR. TEETER: There are also a lot of polls around that tell you what the situation is at a given point in time: You can't have somebody arguing they are going to be happy to get 10 percent when they've already got 25 in the polls.

MR. MEARS: That was a problem in the last campaign. Until 1972 you could count on everybody going around and bragging.

A Homogenized America

MR. SMITH: To come back to the question about the importance of New Hampshire, I think there's one other point besides the one being emphasized, the point Bob Keefe made earlier. There is a much greater connection, a much greater continuum between individual states and the nation as a whole. There isn't that much variation. There is some, but there isn't that much variation. One of the striking things to me in looking at the polls was that at practically the same time the New York Times was doing national polling the Des Moines Register was getting a very similar reading. In the Democratic poll they were getting very similar results to what the national polls were getting, that is, Democratic preferences in Iowa. The Boston Globe was doing its polling up in New Hampshire and also getting fairly similar margins. I don't mean exactly, but if you allow for margins of error, the rough proportions were very similar.

MR. CHAMPION: Let me ask an additional question. Bob Teeter, were the polls elsewhere behaving the same way the polls were in Iowa, say in the Republican race?

MR. TEETER: To a significant degree, yes. There are two points. One is, in 1976, if I'm not mistaken, if I recall it right, from about a week or 10 days before New Hampshire until two weeks after New Hampshire when Ford just beat Reagan, I think Reagan dropped either 16 or 18 percent in Florida in about a three-week period as a result of the New Hampshire result. Second, the point made earlier is that a much larger proportion of the information people are getting in all of these individual states are coming from the same places. I don't think it's just that we have a series of national issues; it's the fact that everybody gets the same network news, a lot of the written press is coming from the wire services and syndicated services and all are coming from the same places. A larger and larger share over the last 10 or 20 years is coming from common sources, particularly network news.

MR. SMITH: Also national poll statistics which are being followed very, very closely and being rereported. They are done by Lou Harris, Gallup or whoever, but immediately incorporated in other reportings.

MR. TEETER: This goes to the whole point you mentioned earlier about personal campaigning. It doesn't matter whether George Bush is standing in Nashua, New Hampshire, or Phoenix; if he's on the network news, he's in your living room.

MR. MEARS: There's a difference on television, there's a big difference on the AP wire, there's a difference in newspapers. If he's in Phoenix, the voter in Nashua may see 30 seconds of him. If he's in Nashua, that voter is going to learn an awful lot more and an awful lot more detailed information about what he said that day and did that day. They are going to see and read 10 times as much.

MR. KEEFE: How?

MR. TEETER: From the barber shop. He's going to dominate the local newspaper.

MR. GRANDMAISON: You also have the situation in downtown Nashua, as an example, that a candidate is scheduled there—he can shake a thousand hands and talk to a thousand people, and it means something in a community of 70,000 people. That candidate can go out and win active supporters, go out and carry that message to their families. There's a multiplication factor that's terribly important to any candidate when it comes to local momentum.

Timing, Momentum and Psychology

MR. CHAMPION: There's also the question of somebody in Phoenix not having a chance to do something about his opinion for several months hence, and it's not quite that close an issue for him as it is for the people immediately in front of it.

We have sort of personalized the New Hampshire primary in a way on the Democratic side—what the issues are and how people looked at those issues. Let's get the Republican situation in New Hampshire on the table—what people think its significance is, how things are going to be read if Reagan finishes ahead of Bush or vice versa. If Baker or somebody else moves up, how much does he need to move up? How are you going to decide those questions as you start to address how you're going to report in New Hampshire?

MR. SMITH: You have raised some of the fundamental questions: Is Ronald Reagan going to come out on top again? Was Iowa a fluke or indicative of a long-term decline for Mr. Reagan? Is it going to be a two-man race or a three-man race? Will Howard Baker suddenly come up, or Anderson come out of nowhere? As you approach the primary, the event itself, your reporting begins to give you a sense of how that's moving. The event itself doesn't occur in isolation, it occurs as part of a continuum.

MR. NELSON: It's certainly not as good as the Democratic case, simply because you have more candidates. For example, no matter how Connally does in New Hampshire, I think he's still alive because he has picked South Carolina, he has strength in other southern primaries. If Baker does very poorly, though, I would think Baker will be fast sliding out of the picture.

MR. MEARS: It wasn't very long ago that other Republicans, notably Connally, were trying to set up Reagan in New Hampshire by saying if he didn't get 50 percent of the vote up there he was a loser because he (Reagan) just about got 50 percent against an incumbent president last time. Connally conveniently didn't mention that it was in a two-man race, instead of a six-man race. As is the case with Kennedy, the fact that Reagan has now been beaten and is no longer allegedly going to march through everything, we have a situation where if he wins he wins. I don't think you play percentage games with Reagan any more. His people have learned their lesson, and the other candidates can't bring it off because he's been beaten.

MR. KEEFE: If he comes in second with approximately the same numbers to anybody in New Hampshire, what does that do?

MR. MEARS: It hurts him.

MR. KEEFE: You don't see him as the guy coming in second, as the Mo Udall of the Republicans?

MR. NELSON: I would think it would hurt him badly.

MR. TEETER: That's not a result of reporting. That's the result of the results.

MR. KEEFE: The presidential campaign is a sequential event in which momentum is everything, is that right?

MR. MEARS: Essentially, yes, at this point. As I said way back, I think that changes at a later stage. As Carter proved last time, you can start losing like crazy.

MR. KEEFE: He kept winning on every day there was a primary.

MR. MEARS: And lost every contested primary he entered after Pennsylvania.

MR. KEEFE: You say contested. He ran uncontested in most of the primaries and picked up delegates everywhere.

MR. MEARS: That's right.

MR. KEEFE: He won a primary every time they had one.

MR. MEARS: After Pennsylvania the process became just reaping delegates up. He did very well, was in it everywhere.

MR. KEEFE: All of that was a product of his early momentum.

MR. MEARS: But if momentum and psychology and all that had been all that important when Jerry Brown started beating him—

MR. KEEFE: It was, because the prologue that set the whole stage was there.

MR. TEETER: That's a perfectly legitimate thing to happen.

MR. KEEFE: It is what had happened before Jerry Brown got in that controlled Jerry Brown's success or failure, because it didn't matter, Carter had it.

MR. MEARS: Put those late primaries first and let Brown beat Carter five times before Pennsylvania and, you know . . .

MR. CHAMPION: Most interestingly, you really left the West out of the process.

MR. KEEFE: They left themselves out by having late processes.

MR. SMITH: Jerry Brown had not filed delegate slates in most of those states. So even when he won the beauty contest, he didn't get the delegates, so Jimmy Carter was still picking up the delegates even when Jerry Brown was winning the popular vote. That was his decision as a candidate. He's not doing it this time. He's getting delegate slates in New York at the same time he's campaigning in New Hampshire and Maine. He got delegates filed in Illinois. It may not be meaningful if he doesn't do well here, but he's in a position where he can reap the benefits of the early part of the game. When you're focusing on the early part of the game, you can't ignore the later part of the game. You've got to take money, put resources in. You've got to get delegate slates.

MR. KEEFE: Which is what Carter did very well last time.

Evaluating the Mix

MR. CHAMPION: Let's pull back just a little bit from the mechanics of the campaign and who is and isn't good at it. Does it serve the country well in terms of having the President in effect nominated before the western part of the country has had a chance to express its opinion?

MR. SMITH: I think not, and I also think, as I said early on in the discussion, that there ought to be some of the larger industrial states, maybe southern states, in the early mix.

MR. TEETER: If you take the first round of the primaries through Illinois, you get at least one major northern state. You get southern states, some eastern states and one large northern industrial state. There are no western states in that mix. I view it from Iowa to Illinois as kind of the end of Round 1. At that point it expands.

MR. KEEFE: It seems that there's only one western state in the whole process, California.

MR. MEARS: Before the McGovern process changed the rules, actually for both parties, because Republicans had to fall in line with Democratic reform when state legislatures started changing their laws to conform with those rules—before that California was pretty crucial; save everything for California.

MR. TEETER: Those legislatures set their own dates.

MR. CHAMPION: We are entitled to ask questions about whether they were wise.

MR. MEARS: Being last had a great advantage to California for quite a while.

MR. CHAMPION: And in some situations might still have. The Los Angeles Times did a very interesting poll asking people how they react to the primaries. The public generally, somewhat on a sliding scale with respect to education and income, think this process is fine, the more the merrier. Do you think it's fine? Do you think it's getting better? Do you think it's getting worse? In terms of serving the country and getting the best candidates nominated, in getting the right kinds of discussion of the issues, is the New Hampshire primary a contributor or not very satisfactory?

MR. SMITH: I'm afraid the trend is going in the wrong direction too fast. We had how many primaries back in the 1960s, but the number is growing rapidly, and if it keeps growing at the rate we are now, we will have not 35 or 36 primaries as we have this year, we will have in the 40s and then move toward a national primary.

MR. KEEFE: The only difference between a caucus and a primary is the length of time the polls are open, really. The process is the same. You divide it proportionately. A caucus today is not like a caucus of 1964.

MR. TEETER: Iowa really was a functional primary. There are all kinds of primaries. I agree with Rick Smith that it's going too fast. I'd rather see a greater mix of ways for people to pick delegates. The Los Angeles Times Poll shows that, even though the process may appear not very tidy and messy and confusing and circus-like at times, the public is reasonably satisfied. They think these individual events are okay.

MR. SMITH: I wonder what would happen if what Bob Keefe suggested earlier happens—if we got this fast sequence, a trend was established, and even before Illinois both races were somehow decided. You would have a very fast operation here, and everything else would be really mechanics of cleaning up. Whether or not in fact the public would feel that way, a number of people in a number of states, large states, would begin to think they were disenfranchised in the presidential process, particularly in the West and even in the Midwest.

MR. NELSON: The reason the public maybe likes this system is because they are getting to see more of the candidates. The candidates are out there, they are tested in a way they haven't really been tested before. I'm not sure having a lot of primaries is that bad. I hear a lot of talk about the wear and tear on the candidates. I think a man who wants to be President, maybe he ought to get out there have a little wear and tear on him. Maybe the people ought to see him. Maybe that's the reason the polls show that the people like this system. They are seeing more of the candidates than they saw back when all of the nominating was done in closed rooms.

MR. TEETER: There's a much greater desire on the part of people like us to want to kind of tidy it up and organize the system better than the public would like to have it. The whole democratic process in this country has never been a particularly tidy thing, or well organized, but it has worked reasonably well. The public understands that and thinks that's what goes on with the primary.

MR. CHAMPION: Including the long season, the kind of period of time in which increasingly there's only politics and very little government?

MR. TEETER: That trend has already reached its culmination.

MR. MEARS: The President says we are only getting government by politics now.

MR. CHAMPION: It is the subject of interpretation.

MR. GRANDMAISON: What we are coming down with is that we think the quantity of primaries is good, that that direction is important to continue, is that correct? Obviously, if not, what we are endorsing, going back to endorsing ward bosses?

MR. SMITH: I don't think so. I think the notion that there was a mix of processes—

MR. GRANDMAISON: Mix of ward bosses would be satisfactory, caucuses.

MR. CHAMPION: You didn't grow up in Michigan or Minnesota or Wisconsin.

MR. GRANDMAISON: What we had in those states before the primary and/or caucus system that is terribly open, as you suggested, was a few people participating in the nominating of the President. We can't just have it both ways. We can't say, gee, there are too many people and it makes it too hard for candidates and too hard for reporters and really too lengthy. I think most people are far brighter than we are. They don't pay a terrible amount of attention to this. Rick Smith tells me New Hampshire voters—I don't know who he's speaking to—are more aware. But I don't believe that every voter is quite as well informed and articulate on the issues as perhaps I got from Rick's suggestion.

MR. SMITH: I said in those states, they were a heck of a lot, are more so, in Iowa and New Hampshire, than in other states. I was amazed coming from Washington—thinking about that and hearing and reading a great deal about the cynicism of Americans with the political process and disinterest—to find as many people as interested as they were.

We are talking about whether Iowa and New Hampshire were sufficiently representative of the country, and the point that I was making was that they were remarkably involved. If 20 percent are actively involved a year before the election of a President, I think that's rather remarkable.

Credibility and the Media

MR. CHAMPION: We have talked about the New Hampshire primary for well over an hour without anybody mentioning Bill Loeb or the Manchester Union-Leader or really any of the questions about whether there are special media influences at play. Somebody said earlier they thought the Boston media now are a major force in New Hampshire election. Do you all agree with that or is that not the case? Or, does Loeb still make any difference?

MR. GRANDMAISON: First, yes, Loeb does make a difference, absolutely no question about it. It's really to a great extent a minimal difference. We participated in a primary for special U.S. Senate race and in a poll that revealed that 45 percent of the people who purchased the Manchester Union-Leader didn't believe what they read in the Union-Leader, meaning that they either had the option of buying it to get some statewide news or not having any statewide news, that simple.

MR. CHAMPION: Wouldn't most political figures settle for having 55 percent belief?

MR. SMITH: That's a general media problem.

MR. GRANDMAISON: What happens is it presumes, if you know a little bit about New Hampshire, that we have some very, very good local newspapers, both dailies as well as weeklies. That means a good campaign recognizes communities where the Union-Leader has a disproportionate share of interest influence over people, meaning the greater Manchester area and towns that do not have immediate access to a daily newspaper. There's no question the Boston media have a tremendous impact, particularly the Globe and television. Boston television is vital to any New Hampshire campaign today. People realized that, I'm sure, back in 1960 or 1956, whatever. The difference is now that the Massachusetts primary is so close in time to the New Hampshire primary, now being a week later, it's just a better business purchase.

MR. KEEFE: When you're talking about why people are buying more Massachusetts media . . .

MR. GRANDMAISON: The spending limit.

MR. KEEFE: Don't forget about the spending limit. You can attribute 16 percent of your buy on television stations to your spending limit in New Hampshire, so you can buy a lot of Boston news.

MR. MEARS: It's always seemed to me Loeb's paper has a great deal more influence in a state contest, particularly a gubernatorial contest, than in any presidential primary or federal election.

MR. GRANDMAISON: It has more influence when indeed it is the only vehicle for communication, obviously. When you pick up Newsweek magazine, they are covering presidential politics: they don't cover gubernatorial races in New Hampshire. That's when it has the influence.

Anybody Loeb is against always has the option of making sure he's going to do something repugnant during this period of that campaign for the candidate he supports, which gets you as many votes as he's taken away from you.

MR. SMITH: Look at the Democratic race this year. You are talking about people who may not choose to use as many of the media options they have. You're talking about greater Manchester, blue-collar people subscribing to the Union-Leader. There might well be an influence. There's been a steady run of articles on Chappaquiddick, on Sen. Kennedy's personal life, a steady series of articles on Mr. Bush.

MR. GRANDMAISON: There's been a steady run of articles in the New York Times on Chappaquiddick. That's not the Union-Leader. That's bad reporting perhaps, whoever is writing it.

MR. SMITH: I don't believe the coverage has been similar. Even if it had been, I think Bob's point is valid. Talking about the voters in New Hampshire and Manchester, we (the New York Times) would love to have that circulation up there, but we don't. There is an impact there. There was an impact on Phil Crane earlier when this happened. It may or may not impact on George Bush. That paper does pick targets.

MR. GRANDMAISON: I would suggest, of course, it does, and there isn't a newspaper today that doesn't pick targets and doesn't somehow give better coverage to some candidates who they tend to support or tend not to support. When you go in and strategize a campaign, you go in the door and say what media are we talking about, who were they for the last time, look at how they covered the race last time and your strategy takes that into account as you develop the plan for that campaign.

MR. CHAMPION: Take a look at the rest of the New Hampshire press. Does it look very much different than the Boston press or in terms of what it covers than the New York Times or what Walter Mears puts on the wire? Or is it pretty much the same? Does it really make any difference in terms of where people are getting their news? Or, is it really that raw impact of television when it first happens that basically is important? In that second opinion, in that series of opinions, is there diversity in it? And we are talking about New Hampshire now.

MR. GRANDMAISON: I would guess that New Hampshire is not any different than the balance of the nation in that respect. The L.A. Times Poll indicates 42 percent of the people say they get a majority of their news from newspapers. Now, I don't know if that's because people don't like to suggest that they get all their news in 30-second actualities, and they like to make people think they subscribe to the New York Times when they don't. But the point is you have that population who say they get in-depth reporting from newspapers.

MR. KEEFE: I worked for a candidate who was an excellent newspaper candidate and he didn't come across too well on television. There is a difference in the impact in the media. I think if you read a report of a Henry M. Jackson speech in 1976 you got a totally different view of what you may have seen on the television, because of the stridency with which he delivered it. That's one of the problems the distinguished senator from this state now has. Had you read, as I did, his speech at Georgetown University, you got one message perhaps you didn't get when you watched it on television, because of the type of delivery, and the type of delivery fits into the whole question of McLuhanesque theories of television. I think that's one of the big differences. They may get their news sources from one place or another, but the impact it has on their heads and where they go with it is very different.

Summing Up

MR. CHAMPION: Let me do one final thing and go around the table and see if you agree with me and have something to add or disagree with me. If I understand what's been said here, first, it's that New Hampshire isn't quite what it used to be, it's a little later on the tour, it isn't quite as important as it was. The second is, it still may be disproportionately important because of where it comes in the timing and sequence and its historic relationship to the process. And finally, that while New Hampshire has got flaws of various kinds, most of you generally don't think it's too bad; that it plays an important role; that the process could be improved. I think it ought to be improved quite substantially in terms of the sequence and timing here if you're going to get an accurate reflection of the electorate.

But most of you don't seem to be very much concerned about that. If I'm wrong, I'd like to hear that. I think finally what everybody seems to say is the success of New Hampshire is that everybody wants to get into the act, that we are going to end up having 50 New Hampshires, that people do want a more open system despite what some students of the process think, some of the people who are players in the process; and that at this point at least they think that process serves, that they see it in the same terms as you see it. I guess I would be more disturbed than the public is that it is such an inside game.

MR. GRANDMAISON: I'm just going to go back and say that I think the most important function that New Hampshire has is that it is a small state that challengers can go into and build a campaign and make their case. Keep in mind that this is a technician speaking. I think the moment that the process doesn't begin in a fashion that allows, whether it be a Bush or a McGovern or a Jimmy Carter four years ago, an opportunity to build momentum, then I think we are all the losers. And if you're concerned about what is best for America, there's nothing worse than if we required our candidates to immediately be funded to the level of a New York or a Pennsylvania campaign, a heavy media effort at four and five thousand dollars for every 30-second television spot. The difference between Connally's investment in New Hampshire—he can't lose in New Hampshire and the reason he can't lose is he's already got enough money to go in South Carolina. What you win or lose in New Hampshire is momentum, the opportunity to gain additional resources, primarily funds.

MR. KEEFE: It's clear that New Hampshire is not as important as it was, not important for two reasons. One, it's not first any more in the process. And second, there's more of the process and it's a smaller part of it. I would agree that it's nice to have early states where you have smaller areas that require a little bit less money, but the candidates this time have done a reasonably good job of getting enough money to go a little ways and maybe that's something that federal funding and so forth has allowed them to do.

But I think that the process as we have developed it is going to be with us for a while. We are really in about the second period of presidential primaries as we now know them; 1972 was still a process of great change when the McGovern rules were coming in and people were switching to primaries in order to keep themselves from being contested in credentials challenges because the caucuses didn't work right. And 1976 sort of was a full-blown, new-process kind of presidential election. So 1980 will be the second time and we will probably have a reasonably similar system for the whole nominating process over the next several presidential elections. I'm sort of anxious to see how this one goes because it's the second in a series that's going to determine who our presidents are over the next 20 years probably, and if we can learn something from this experience, maybe we can do it better next time too.

MR. TEETER: The sequence is what is important. It would be improved if we had a large industrial state and maybe some western states earlier in that sequence. One of the things that Iowa may have been useful for us this year is that we begin to come to the notion that you don't have to have a primary to have an open system and have a system with substantial participation.

There are other ways to have a lot of participation and have it be just as open as having a primary. The whole argument of money is important, and it's important for people who have a situation where they can get started. At the same time there's some direct relationship between money and support. If Bob Dole's campaign is out of money, it's also out of support, and as campaigns gain support, they traditionally gain money. If you could go out and look at the cash receipts in the week after Iowa for all the Republican campaigns, you see that as Bush gained support, he also gained a lot of money. That's something that is always going to be true. It may be important to have a situation where everyone can get started evenly.

MR. MEARS: I would differ with what I think to be the suggestion that this is an insider's process. What we have been talking about all this time is a process not totally available to anyone who wants it. And that creates some of the very problems that we have been discussing. That's why you have 37 primaries. That's where the reform rules led because if you didn't go the primary route you were much more susceptible to being thrown out of the convention. I don't think there's any way of turning that around, nor do I think it should be turned around.

MR. NELSON: I am sort of the odd man out because I like the primary system. I think probably the more primaries, the better. Maybe you ought to have regional primaries, I don't know. But I like the idea that politicians have to go through this testing procedure. It's good for them to be out there for a long time. It's good for us to follow them out there for a long time. That way we find out more about them and the public finds out more about them.

MR. SMITH: I don't think it's an insider's process. I think it's a wide-open process. I'd go back to something Bob Teeter said. Though I like the sequence of primaries, I might jumble the sequence a bit and advocate some kind of mix of primaries and caucuses and district conventions. But I hope we don't go in the direction of large regional primaries because I think we will go from that to a national primary. If we do that, we will rule out challenges to sitting Presidents within their own parties, which has been an important feature of this election and of the last election, and it would make it much more difficult for the new political figures to make the national run.

ROUNDTABLE TWO

Primaries Versus Caucuses

MODERATOR

F. Christopher Arterton is an associate professor of political science at Yale University, with emphasis on American political parties and elections. He also is chairman of a faculty study group at the Institute of Politics that has been examining the financing of election campaigns. Dr. Arterton was a delegate to the 1972 Democratic National Convention and a platform committee member. He also served on the Democratic National Committee's Commission on Party Structure and Delegate Selection (the Winograd Commission), which designed rules for the 1980 national convention. He now is chairman of the Progressive Alliance's Commission on the Political Process.

PANELISTS

James Gannon is executive editor of the Des Moines Register.

Tim Kraft is national campaign manager for the Carter/Mondale Presidential Committee.

James M. Naughton is metropolitan editor of the Philadelphia Enquirer.

Robert Scheer is a national correspondent for the Los Angeles Times.

Richard G. Stearns worked with the campaign of Sen. George McGovern (D-S.D.) in 1972 and is now chief of delegate selection for the Kennedy for President Committee.

F. Clifton White is president of F. Clifton White and Associates, and was national director of the Goldwater for President Committee in 1964, consultant to the chairman of the Committee to Reelect the President in 1972 and an adviser to the President Ford Committee in 1976.

ROUNDTABLE TWO

The Impact of Primaries; Differences in Strategy; The Big Turnout in Iowa; The Parties and the Caucuses; The Issues—Promises and Cynicism; The Press and the Issues; The Effect on Party Building; Working With New Rules; National and Regional Primaries; Trends in Participation; The Value of the Smaller Events; The Importance of Being First; Picking the Best Candidate; The Press as Adversary; Summing Up.

The Impact of Primaries

F. CHRISTOPHER ARTERTON: It's quite clear that if there's been a competition between primaries and caucuses, primaries have been winning. In 1956 we had 15 primaries and they selected about 40 percent of the delegates. That is, 60 percent were selected by caucuses or by conventions. In 1972 that number jumped to 22 primaries. It jumped again in 1976 to 30 primaries. And by my count this time we are up to 34 Democratic primaries and 35 Republican primaries. These primaries apportion 76 and 78 percent of the delegates respectively. Now, the growth in those numbers of primaries has changed the strategies of the contestants, and by contestants, I mean participants, both the contestants and the news media. Now campaigns must reach toward a larger audience, a larger electorate. They are not running a quiet campaign anymore to garner commitments of delegates that select themselves. Rather, they are trying to elect their own delegates. It's not an effort any more to obtain the support of a few people who control delegates; rather, it's an attempt to get your own people to the convention through running in these primaries. Caucuses, however, still play an important part of the process. In 1972 George McGovern did better in the caucuses than he did in the more visible primaries. That is, he had a higher percentage of those caucus delegates than he had of the primary delegates. In 1976, however, Carter did better in the primaries than he did in the caucuses. He picked up 42 percent of the primary delegates and only 32 percent of the caucus delegates.

We heard our participants in Roundtable No. 1 assert that caucuses have this time become the functional equivalent of primaries, spurred mostly by comments about Iowa, where turnout jumped from nine or 10 percent in 1976 up to 25 percent two weeks ago. But people still participate much less in caucuses, and that raises the question of which of these systems is better than the other, more representative and so forth.

Let's start off by getting into a discussion of these two systems from the vantage point of campaign managers. I'd like to ask Tim Kraft and Rick Stearns first if they could talk about what differences they employ in how they go about getting delegates and getting people involved in the process in caucuses versus primaries. What are the differences in what you do?

Differences in Strategy

TIM KRAFT: I would say with regard to our situation in Iowa, both the last time and this time around, there is a difference in strategy. It's a caucus state. And the emphasis is on securing individual commitments and extending a very personal, committed network of Iowans in that particular state to participate in their campaign and asking them to multiply their efforts by enlisting other Iowans for the same effort to pull on the caucus night. To secure this sort of commitment we don't employ the sort of media campaigns and crowd-building exercises which you would in a primary state. It is required of a candidate that he go into the state, that he deal with people in small groups, that he explain his position in some detail, that he secure his commitment and keep in touch with the people and that he have a staff that's prepared to do that. And to the extent that you have indigenous support working on your candidate's behalf, he will do well in the campaigns. Caucuses are not susceptible to media campaigns or outside blitzes.

RICHARD G. STEARNS: I probably would say the same thing perhaps slightly differently. You have two different exercises you pursue in a political campaign. One is identification of your own vote and the other is persuasion of an undefined vote. In a caucus state where you're dealing with a much smaller rate of participation, the identification of your vote is the more important. That means that devices like telephones, direct mail response and personal voter contact are more important to the campaign manager than the persuasive devices that the mass media generally provide. So it does influence your strategy, does influence what you use. You're looking for a much smaller group, and it has to be a group at the end of the process that is far more highly motivated than the typical voter that takes part in the primary. You're asking people to do something that is for most people's experience an abnormal act which requires a high degree of commitment. You're asking him to go into a neighbor's living room and disagree with someone they have to live with for the rest of the year and not be protected by the anonymity of the voting booth.

MR. ARTERTON: It seemed to me from what you were saying that you required much more intensive effort to organize a primary state than a caucus state. Is that right? If so, are you looking further down the calendar? Are you working on Wisconsin now? Are you working on Pennsylvania?

MR. STEARNS: I would say just the reverse. It's less of an effort in the sense you mean organizing a primary state. That requires production of some television film by making media buys. That is what you're looking to do in the long-range sense of the word. Organizing for the caucus once you identify motivation to participate in a very small kind of meeting requires a great deal of exposure for the campaign, a great deal more organization in the traditional political sense than a primary state requires. With enough money, I think you could organize almost any of either party's primaries in a relatively short period of time.

The Big Turnout in Iowa

ROBERT SCHEER: Do you think the Carter people are manipulating the election right now? Do you think they are milking the international problem, and do you think it matters as far as their ability to manipulate in a primary or caucus?

MR. STEARNS: The line between manipulation and persuasion in politics is a very difficult one to draw. In Iowa there clearly was a phenomenon at work which has very little to do with any of the rules of caucuses or primaries that I know from my own experience. The injection of the international crisis into the campaign clearly influenced the voter turnout in Iowa. That was a phenomenal turnout if it was 25 percent. That would suggest that it was four times higher than any previous Iowa caucus I can think of, except perhaps in 1968, when you had somewhat the same phenomenon when again a war situation injected itself into the caucuses. In 1968 I think 78,000 was the best estimate that I read.

JAMES GANNON: I don't think you can explain the Iowa turnout by Iran and Afghanistan. I really think that was almost irrelevant. What happened in Iowa was that people got caught up in something that became the national Super Bowl, the kickoff of the campaign. And people got intensely interested because there was a televised debate, there was a big flap over a nondebate, Carter/Kennedy, and all of a sudden Walter Cronkite and John Chancellor were there and this great big circus was going on and people decided hey, this is fun, let's be part of it. The turnout was mostly not the organizational politics working, but a much more spontaneous thing. I mean I'd be interested in hearing whether Tim Kraft agrees with that. There were an awful lot of walk-ins that you guys didn't know about before that evening.

MR. KRAFT: That's right. Also the Iowa Democratic electorate, and the Republican as well, has been building up to this. In 1972 there was a lot of organizational activity. In 1976 there were five Democratic candidates in the state and four had very aggressive campaigns. This is the third presidential election with an increasing amount of national attention paid to that state. There's a civic awareness and pride there that responded accordingly.

JAMES M. NAUGHTON: If the Iowa caucus were in April, I don't think they would have had anywhere near the attention paid to it—nor the kind of participation.

MR. GANNON: No doubt, absolutely right.

F. CLIFTON WHITE: There's participation by virtue of its being first. I also think some of the participation that Tim is talking about is educating people to the fact they can participate. One of our problems has been that people did not really know or believe that their participation was going to be meaningful in the political process, therefore, why bother to go do it. This kept building up and, as a result of all the attention, everybody, certainly almost everybody in Iowa, knew when the caucuses were going to take place. I expect you find a few people who didn't but most of them did. On that basis you increase the participation above that level of the professional group that normally would attend the caucus situation.

MR. ARTERTON: Is that to say that the early discussion that they had about the differences in their strategies in caucuses versus primaries, you can turn almost any caucus into a primary if you wanted to, if you wanted to devote the resources?

MR. WHITE: I'm not sure that we could do it as politicians. But if we can get John Chancellor and Walter Cronkite and all the rest to pay that kind of attention to it, we may be able to turn it into a situation in which you get the same kind of response and interest. If the media says this is *the* caucus or this is *the* state in which the nomination is going to be selected, at that point we will have generated enough interest.

MR. NAUGHTON: We say that about every one of them.

The Parties and the Caucuses

MR. WHITE: I know; they don't believe you all the way down the line. When you get one like the first, one that you can focus on and get an appropriate buildup, then I think it does work. But normally in a caucus state it is not the media, it's more the personal contact, it's more the organizational effort. And I think this is an important point, historically. Caucuses are very important. I personally am disturbed that we have gone so far toward primaries. I think we are overdoing the primary situation, because normally what you would get in a caucus situation are what I would call the professionals, the people who are interested in politics on a yearly basis and pay attention to it. And they go to the caucuses for the purpose of discussion—or used to go for the purpose of trying to find a candidate that they think would fit their constituency and fit their party.

Now, today we are getting to where we are making our conventions almost computer printouts. I mean you can watch CBS and know what's going to happen before the convention occurs, so they say, because of commitments, because of primaries and all the rest. It's very important in the nominating process that you have a group of people who are concerned with the political process participating in a discursive way about who their candidates are going to be.

MR. NAUGHTON: If it's true that it's a different process to organize a caucus, and it's less expensive—you don't have the big media buys, you don't have the big overhead of running the candidate and a whole train of people in as often as happens in a primary state—and if it does get more people involved, why are the professionals allowing the primaries to take over?

MR. WHITE: Primaries are an easy way to get out of the problem of having good organization and, of course, what's been happening in the last 10 or 15 years concomittantly with the change in the nominating process has been the decline in influence of the political parties, the parties themselves.

But the parties were the ones that used to produce the people who came to the caucuses. Now the parties are so weak—and yet most party leaders don't want to admit they are weak—the answer is to turn it over to the public in terms of the primary, and the other answer is the primaries have been sold as being more democratic.

MR. STEARNS: I don't want to let this point go by. I don't think we should let Walter Cronkite get away with his influence this easily. This is not the first time that the Iowa caucuses were either in any sense of the word first or well covered. I have some experience with the Iowa caucuses going back to 1968, less so in 1976, but certainly in 1972 and certainly this time. The caucuses were covered prior to the event of 1972 and the event itself was covered not only by the print media, but by television as well. In 1976, everybody will agree, the Iowa caucuses were heavily covered and gave President Carter his start. In 1980 they were more intensely covered. This has been a growing process.

There were intensive organizational efforts mounted in the state by McGovern in 1972 and Carter in 1976 and both times the turnout was roughly the same, 7 to 8 percent.

In 1980 it was probably the most intensively organized Democratic campaign. I'm sure it was true on the Republican side as well. I know what we had organized—that is, what the Kennedy campaign had organized in the state—and I have a good idea what was actually organized by President Carter's campaign.

If it had been left to a pure organizational effort, I think we would have turned out about 14 percent of the electorate in the Democratic caucuses. Somewhere an extra 10 percent materialized. The only other time I have seen that phenomenon happen was in 1968 where again you had an unorganized extra 30,000 or 40,000—it was a smaller Democratic electorate then—spontaneously appear at the caucuses. Aside from the media attention—I don't mean to say there is no influence that Cronkite and so on inject into the situation—the two common factors were a war. The Vietnam War in 1968, which brought a lot of unorganized people spontaneously into the caucuses, and in 1980 a looming war in the Persian Gulf which I think had exactly the same effect. I think it's too simple to simply say that the prospect of seeing yourself on national television or have Adam Clymer write about you in the New York Times is what brings out this extra 40,000 or 50,000 people.

MR. GANNON: If there was a great Iowa fear of war or anything like 1968, we certainly totally missed it. I don't see how you can compare 1980 and 1968 in Iowa. There's no great big antiwar uprising in Iowa.

The Issues: Promises and Cynicism

MR. SCHEER: This is what interests me about this. Why isn't there? Why isn't there more of a concern about the issues? The question of primary versus caucuses is only interesting insofar as it tells you whether democracy works better or not, whether important matters are discussed. You look at Iowa. I don't think it matters terribly whether it's a primary or caucus. What was missing in Iowa was not a technical question of the details of the game; what was missing was a serious debate of whether we should go back to 1950 and the Cold War.

MR. GANNON: We tried to have a debate.

MR. SCHEER: The most serious thing that happened so far as the President is concerned is his refusal to participate—and Ronald Reagan's refusal to participate. The question should be raised about both primaries and caucuses—how do you have more serious debate of the issues? A question has to be raised about the media and its ability to cover these things. I would be in favor of grouping them regionally just because you can get at the candidate. I think we should address ourselves to why is there so much cynicism about campaigning. Maybe you can enlighten us. When we cover a campaign—press, campaign workers and candidates get terribly cynical about the whole process. Issues become things you throw out there. For instance, let's take Carter in Iowa and New Hampshire last time. He was against the three-martini lunch, he was against the country club set, he was a populist. He promised them: you will not see the same faces in Washington, you'll never see the Cy Vances and Zbigniew Brzezinskis in Washington, it's going to be a new crowd. That was so much garbage. These guys were already on the plane, already writing speeches. You have George Bush running around Iowa as if he were some small-town Texas populist—"When my wife and I are down there barbecuing, it's just like in Plains." We know that's not George Bush. We know him as a rather established conventional candidate. I think there's a process of deception involved in these things and we should discuss why that happens and whether it happens less in caucuses or in primaries and what to do about it.

MR. KRAFT: Your preoccupation with deception and manipulation and cynicism—all the downside of the nomination and delegate selection processes—is obvious. But the fact of the matter is, Bob, I don't know how many Iowans you talked to, I don't know how many hours you spent around the kitchen table with people. Our campaign people did a lot of that, and they would talk about the President's record in the past three years, and they would try to answer some of the charges that may have come from the other campaign. I'm sure Kennedy campaign coordinators did the same thing. There is a more qualitative albeit smaller debate about the delegate selection process in Iowa than you give it credit for.

MR. NAUGHTON: To the extent there is a cynicism bred by the phoniness in the process, it's much more likely to occur in a primary situation than in a caucus state.

MR. ARTERTON: Could you push what Tim Kraft was saying to argue that, if issues are not dealt with, they are likely to be not dealt with in primary situations where you're reaching toward a broad audience; and this kind of personal organizing goes on in caucus states where you really have to deal with people and you have to make your pitch based on the issues. The difference is the press may not be able to cover the latter, whereas in the former they can see candidates roaming around and staging media events.

MR. WHITE: That's precisely the point, and it's one of the advantages of the caucuses. People are together. They do not walk through a booth. They sit down in somebody's living room or in the high school auditorium or someplace and there is some kind of discussion. In regard to what issues are debated or discussed in regard to the general public, I would suggest that the media have a great deal to do with saying what they want discussed. As far as I know in any experience I have ever had, there is not a candidate seeking public office who is not anxious to talk to any voter about whatever that voter has got on his mind. And we spend a great deal of time and a great deal of money trying to find out what the heck the voter is worried about and trying to establish a way to talk to him about it. Because we know very well that to get the attention of a voter and, therefore, to be able to persuade him to support our candidate, we've got to talk about something he's interested in, and politics isn't solely enough to get him to listen to us.

You can't walk up to an average citizen, whoever that is, and say, "I'm a politician, I want to talk to you," and get his attention. You've got to go up and talk to him about what he is concerned with and what he's interested in. I think there is more time—and these young active campaign managers, I think, will agree with this—spent on trying to figure out how in the world we can get the voter to listen to us on the basis of the issues that we are concerned about. The cynicism very well can come from what's written in media.

MR. ARTERTON: Rick Stearns, when you are making your pitch in Iowa versus New Hampshire or a larger primary, is it true that you have to be more detailed in what you're talking to these activists about than you really can be when you're running around campaigning through the media?

MR. STEARNS: Communication is a little quieter in caucuses because you're dealing with a smaller, potentially interested electorate. You actually have more time to tailor responses to specific issues. If, for example, you're running a telephone canvas of Des Moines, starting sufficiently early, and someone has a kind of select question that ordinarily he would not address the general electorate with, you can answer it on a telephone. If someone tells you they really want to know what you're going to do about the Chicago Board of Trade, you can answer. That's something in Iowa and most places you wouldn't bother to address to the general electorate, but you can sit down and find some sort of reasoned position explaining exactly what he would or wouldn't do on a question that is that narrowly drawn. Issues communication tends to be much more private and perhaps less visible than it is in the primary state.

The Press and the Issues

MR. ARTERTON: If that's the case, how does the press go about covering issues in caucuses?

MR. SCHEER: The press is always criticized for not covering issues. The reason the press gets bored covering issues is the candidates are playing with the issues. I remember Carter last time out spoke to some rabbis in Los Angeles. He said if he were the prime minister in Israel, he wouldn't give back an inch of the occupied territory. Half-hour later he's for U.N. Resolution 242. You go to Jody Powell and say, how do you square the two? Well, he said if he's the prime minister, but he isn't the prime minister, he's going to be the President of the United States. (Laughter)

When Kennedy came out with that remark about the Shah, the question the press and other candidates should have asked is, is this a accurate comment? This was not discussed. What was discussed was whether this was a dumb move, whether he had screwed up his campaign, was back in the game; did Kennedy stumble, commit an error, was this lousy strategy? The question of whether this statement was accurate, whether this should change our view, was not discussed.

I interviewed Bush before Iowa and he made what I thought was an astounding statement, which we carried in the L. A. Times. He said nuclear war is an option and that you can win a nuclear war. I felt sort of, back to Dr. Strangelove. It wasn't picked up anywhere—I didn't find any great interest in it—because it's not part of the game. What people are more interested in—is he up two percent in the polls, one percent? I found it an astounding statement. I found a story by Jack Nelson in our paper saying that people in the Carter government are contemplating the nuclear option. Pondering the unthinkable. If that's true, why aren't there lots of stories about it, why aren't the other candidates discussing that? If we are moving toward nuclear war, who cares whether you have caucuses or primaries? I want to know whether we should move to nuclear war. That's what I'd like to see the candidates discussing, and that's not being discussed.

MR. ARTERTON: Jim Naughton, is it true the horse race aspects of the primaries are clear? Is that something that means in reporting primaries you tend to focus on those aspects more directly, which would tend to indicate that as primaries have increased we have sort of pushed the press toward covering horse races?

MR. NAUGHTON: The more primaries we have, the more we are forced into a situation where everybody is trying to get a grasp on who is up, who is down, who's sliding, who is rising. We are increasing attention to the mechanics of the system rather than to the substance. I don't think there's any question that's the case. And that's bad.

MR. ARTERTON: Jim, what efforts did you make in Iowa to cover the issues that candidates were really running on as opposed to the horse race things?

MR. GANNON: You know, they really weren't running on issues. We made efforts to present issue stands of each of the candidates, we did all that. But the fact is I don't think issues were terribly important except on the Democratic side. Obviously the situation in Iran, Afghanistan, everything else, had an important effect in that you tended to submerge other issues. But it wasn't that candidates were going around saying here, these are my key issues and this is really important and people were listening to that. I think it was much more just like in a primary state—the perception of the candidate, the personality—is Reagan too old, is Kennedy a man of character, is Carter competent. Those were the questions that I think voters were really dealing with. Not is Kennedy's stand on national health insurance more sensible than Carter's. I just don't think you have that kind of issue engagement in a very detailed sense.

MR. NAUGHTON: We have people at this table who worked for candidates who got very heavily into issue engagement in past years, and McGovern's experience and Goldwater's experience probably tell candidates not to risk that kind of discussion. You may want to speak to that, Cliff.

MR. WHITE: Sure, that's partly true. And the problem when you get involved in the complicated issue, particularly in the period of the campaign itself, is to have the ability to develop it and carry it on with a thorough full-scale discussion of the issue, because your activists and those so-called people and voters out there really don't want you to go that far. They want you to give them that simple one paragraph statement that says I'm for or against A, B, or C, that they can then take out and promote. And it doesn't end up being a good campaign procedure. Only a relatively few people—and a large percentage of those don't bother to vote in the primary—are really going to follow you through in a detailed, very detailed aggressive discussion of the issues. I don't know when or how this started. It's really the horse race aspect of our campaign, the amount of time and money that the media spends trying to figure out who is going to win or who does win in each area that is just fantastic today. We have turned this whole thing into a question of deciding who is ahead at point A or B or who is winning this number of delegates, and we try to get the delegates locked in earlier and committed, and we have actually changed the whole character of the national nominating convention.

Originally they were deliberative bodies, really. You can call them smoke-filled rooms, call them evil and sinister and everything else, but there was a group of people that went to those conventions and sat down and very seriously tried to figure out who was going to be the best nominee and what were the issues upon which he ought to run. We have changed that. I don't advocate exclusive caucuses. I think what we need is a mix of primaries and caucuses, but one of the advantages of the caucuses actually is that it is more difficult for the media to interfere. They can't interview 5,000 precinct caucuses in Iowa; they can't all be there at that time.

MR. NAUGHTON: Are we in a caucus state likely to get a more genuine discussion of the issues? I frankly doubt it. I think the candidates don't want it.

MR. WHITE: I'm not sure you get a totally better discussion of the issue. But you do get a better discussion of the campaign and the personality and the interrelationship of people in contrast to what I feel you tend to get more in the primary states where you get the interrelationship of technology.

MR. ARTERTON: Do you feel you get better reporting in caucuses?

MR. WHITE: No.

MR. ARTERTON: Worse?

MR. WHITE: Worse, worse. Because it's more difficult. It's much more difficult. It's a lot easier to report a primary. You can sit there with your charts and scales and take your surveys as they leave the polls. You can at least project to the national television audience anything you want to after a primary.

I mean you can even decide what issues were decided in that primary by just picking out which questions you're going to ask the people when they leave the poll. Were you interested in potholes on your street this morning? That will show up as a 90 percent issue in a primary in a given state if you, the surveyor, asked that question. Or you can ask is it important what's going on in Iran. Sure, 90 percent of them will say yes. You can write all your stories.

In a caucus state you get a discussion. Gee, I really had trouble with my neighbor this week about the fact that the price of grain may have gone down. What are we going to do about that? And then some local leader takes that on up and finally gets to Tim Kraft or somebody and says hey, you got to give us an answer. That's not an in-depth discussion of the issue. But it's the kind of discussion that's going to be meaningful and going to persuade somebody to vote for your candidate.

The Effect on Party Building

MR. GANNON: I don't think the quality or type of reporting out of Iowa would have been any different if it had been a primary. I just don't see that it matters that you get poorer reporting out of a caucus state, unless you're talking about reporting election results being a little more difficult. But the candidates would have been doing the same thing had it been a primary. Their organizations would have been doing some different, I suppose, for the media. It seems to me Iowa almost blended the thing. We got sort of a combined caucus-primary thing with the turnout and the media attention. John Connally was in there playing television commercials like it was a primary state, and the candidates were all campaigning like it was New Hampshire. I think the distinction blurs a great deal. Except for one thing—its effect afterward on party building.

The real value of the caucus is you get this hundred thousand people who come out, they get involved in politics maybe for the first time, and half of them or a third of them or some number of them are going to stick with it and be interested in it, be the great pool of new blood for the parties. That's the long-range good thing about the caucus.

MR. ARTERTON: Do you think that's right? There are likely to be Kennedy people and Carter people who turned out at those caucuses. Are they really primarily Kennedy people, Carter people, or are they going to turn out to be party people after this?

MR. STEARNS: A lot of them were party people before they became Carter people or Kennedy people in terms of the 1980 caucuses. I generally agree. Caucuses serve a different value than primaries do from a party's point of view. The caucus is probably a healthier mechanism for developing the party as an institution. It does not register public sentiment on a given issue or candidate as well as a primary vote does simply because a primary vote is larger in the canvass. Not only does some discussion take place at the first level of the caucus, but it's an ongoing process in Iowa. We have some 7,000 people attending county conventions and eventually 3,000 convene in district and state meetings.

This is over a period of time. It's a discussion that will get relatively more refined as the group winnows itself out. But it still is a party discussion basically. A lot of people knew each other before the process began, but a lot of new people are going to find themselves caught up in this process and carry it to some conclusion, and I think in the end they will emerge as Democrats much as they will partisans to a given candidate.

MR. GANNON: Do you think the outcome in Iowa would have been any different on the Democratic side had it been a primary?

MR. KRAFT: Carter would have made a good showing in a primary as well. Another assist that this kind of turnout and commitment around the state gives your campaign is a leg up from the general election. Again, I go back to persuasion and the one-on-one and the personal effort you have to make to get your friend or associate or colleague or neighbor to go to a caucus. If he'll give of himself at that time for two or three hours on a Monday night, he may be interested enough to follow the delegate selection process up through the state convention.

I agree with Cliff White that in the national scheme of things, the candidate selection process, a mix of caucuses and primaries is a healthy thing. Rick Stearns would agree with me that I would shrink at the prospect of organizing caucuses in California or New York—large states that are probably better served by primaries.

MR. NAUGHTON: Is it that the states are better served by primaries or that the candidates are in those states?

MR. KRAFT: A caucus process exacts a lot on the state party as well. They have to go through all the process of notification and selection of the sites and the conducting of the business and tabulation of the results. I'm not so sure some of the state parties in the larger states would welcome the rigors of a caucus.

Working With New Rules

MR. NAUGHTON: Isn't one of the reasons we have fewer and fewer caucus states that the rules are so much more difficult to carry out in a caucus, the balancing of the delegates? You can manipulate a primary situation as a candidate a lot more readily than you can a caucus situation, and as a party it's much easier to manage.

MR. KRAFT: I don't agree with that. I don't think there's a manipulation factor that's relevant either in caucus or primary in terms of the candidate or delegate selection. Even in a primary situation you have the same requirements of affirmative action for the Democratic Party, equal division and other reform rules and provisions that the party must execute. In terms of the rules and reforms, I don't see how that makes the caucus versus primary that much easier or for a primary candidate or a party.

MR. STEARNS: The myth is that the difficulty the state governments had making new rules was the reason a number of states adopted primaries. The fact is the Democratic Party rules are incomprehensible either in a caucus or primary situation. The reason the shift occurred after 1972 is because McGovern frankly out-organized the regular party in a lot of states. They resented it and thought they would do better in a primary.

A second reason was New Hampshire having an early primary. A lot of states didn't understand New Hampshire's success depended on its being first, and states like Nevada and New Mexico to an extent adopted primaries in hopes it would bring Walter Cronkite to the state along with the rest of the traveling press.

Let me suggest one very important reason why we have to maintain the mix and hope, as long as the campaign finance laws last, that the number of caucuses will continue to grow. It is much cheaper to organize a caucus campaign than a primary campaign. In a state like Virginia with 10 congressional districts I could run an effective caucus campaign on a budget of about $80,000.

In the last Senate campaign in the State of Virginia, both candidates spent more than a million dollars on their nomination races alone. The present law allows us a ceiling expenditure effectively this year of 13, 14 million dollars that we can spend in actually running a campaign.

If we have to look at the prospect of taking that $13 million and dividing it up among 50 states, there are 10 major primaries each of which could reasonably—I don't mean excessively—reasonably spend a million dollars on television alone. The more primaries there are, the more expensive the process gets for us, the less money we have to allocate. It comes to the point where you're beginning to talk about a media budget in a state like Illinois or New York of $250,000 that really is nothing in terms of the candidate's ability to communicate an independent message to the voters.

One of the consequences of the campaign finance laws that was overlooked at the time—and I'll not try to place a value judgment on whether it was a good or bad thing—was really to shift the power of carrying the message from the candidate himself to the news media. We made the news media the most powerful actor in the nomination process. Even a John Connally can't really go around what the New York Times or the evening news or Los Angeles Times or any other paper is saying about him. You cannot raise the money nor can you spend it under these laws to carry your own message directly to the voters.

So you have to begin thinking of ways to influence the press to carry the message for you. You have to somehow beguile or trap the media into doing for you what you can't pay for yourselves.

National and Regional Primaries

MR. SCHEER: I want to be constructive, so let me say my suggestion would be to get rid of the endless primaries, have regional or national primaries, put a major emphasis on debates. I think that Republican debate in Iowa was marvelous, one of the best things that's happened in recent history. Put more emphasis on that, pressure or require candidates to show up at these things.

There's a special problem with the drawn out system of primaries and caucuses. What it allows is for an unknown to get in. These people do not have a track record. They don't have 12 years in the Senate and five in the House. They don't have things you can hang them with. Dole gets out there and we can go through the clips, say wait a minute, you were for this, you were against this, are you changing. Kennedy is having that problem. He's got a track record. You can confront him with it. You got a guy like Carter and you wrap him up, or get a guy like Caddell or Rafshoon wrapping him up, he doesn't have anything you can pin him on except some myths about what went on in Georgia.

By the time you unravel that and find out some of the reality, the election is over anyway. You're running around with this image of yourself. I don't think it's particularly democratic. You hear the small meetings, so forth, Jimmy Carter getting up time after time and saying, I want a government that's as meaningful, warm, lovely, blah, blah, blah, blah, blah as you are and smiling and going on to the next shopping center. I don't find that's a terribly interesting exercise.

MR. KRAFT: If your readership is subject to the same objectivity and dispassionate analysis (Laughter and applause) that you are demonstrating here today, I'm afraid we are going to have to take a full page ad in the paper regardless of what it costs.

MR. ARTERTON: Rick Stearns said a moment ago that we have systematically infused the news media into a vital role in the process. Now, that being the case, these people want to use the news media to get their message out to the people who are going to support them. They can't do it themselves, they don't have enough money to do it, they need you to do it. Are you saying you don't think that's a healthy process, that we ought to go back to more party process, a more personal contacting process in which—we had some agreement on that—we are going to get more of a debate of the issues? Here you are sitting as a gate keeper and you don't seem to think like it.

MR. SCHEER: I made some very specific suggestions. I don't think it's an inherently democratic process to have these endless primaries, media events, so forth. I think regional primaries, some way of tidying it up, would be better. Put the emphasis on debates, on serious discussion.

First of all, I disagree with the notion that the public is not interested in issues. My experience with these candidates is that the public is interested. You go up to Oregon, they have a lot of questions about the environment. You go to Iowa, there are serious questions about farm policy and inflation and so forth. I think the public as well as the press gets tired of trying to follow the issues because they don't really believe you are going to tell them what you're going to do. Everyone is against inflation, all candidates come before you and say they are against inflation. They all say they are going to balance the budget. They all say they are going to keep you out of war. You go right down the line. The public gets tired of it.

MR. WHITE: Don't you think they believe that? Don't you think they want to do those things? Don't you think every candidate running for office, whether it be President of the United States, senator or governor, does want to do something about inflation, does want to keep us out of war? Of course they want to.

The question is what they are going to do. They are not going to be in a position to make an absolute judgment on that until they hold the office, until they face the circumstances, until they find out what's going on. I think the American people understand that. I don't think the American people have the problem. I think some of it may be a problem with the interpreters to the American people in some cases as to what they are trying to tell the American people they ought to be thinking about or the issue they ought to be concerned with.

Let the people talk. Let the candidates get out and meet with the people. You'll find that the people and the opposing candidates, if you have a truly competitive operation, are going to force the candidates to positions or, if not, to the failure to adopt a position, which the public is going to perceive.

MR. GANNON: I can't see that your solution is a solution of the problem at all. It makes it worse.

MR. SCHEER: It's a step in the right direction.

MR. GANNON: No, a step in the wrong direction, because if you go to a regional or national primary you aren't going to get discussion of issues, but big media campaigns. You aren't going to get any discussion of an agriculture issue. When the campaigns come to Iowa there are people there who ask them what they are going to do about farm problems. They have to answer that, and there is a record established or some notion what they're all about. You aren't going to have that if you have a western regional primary or even a midwestern primary and you certainly aren't going to have it in a national primary. You're going to get a big television campaign and that's all and everything else is irrelevant.

Trends in Participation

MR. WHITE: I have been through a lot of politics in the last 30 years. I think one of the most exciting things that happened was the caucus vote in Iowa, the size of it. To me one of the things that says is that the American people are beginning to pull out a little bit of their frustration, their cynicism, their belief that it doesn't make any difference, that they can't have an impact. That in effect the system with all the tinkering—and this is what the

L.A. Times Poll is also suggesting—that the system, with all the tinkering we have done with it, with all of the errors that many of us think exist, is there. And I would suggest that both the politicians this year and the media this year have a responsibility to try to capitalize on this involvement factor and pull up the involvement of people into the democratic process. And this will come both with the primaries and with the caucuses both as we go down the road. That's why I think the Iowa debate is the first debate I have seen in this whole business in which, sure, people tried to pick a winner, but it was not really who won or who lost, it was a presentation of candidates trying to discuss the issues.

I think that's a very good thing. And I think rather than having this gamesmanship, if we can get back here to the involvement which will come from both caucus and primary states in a proper mix, then you're going to start making the system be a good deal more effective.

And my judgment of Iowa is that the public in Iowa at least is less frustrated than Bob Scheer in regard to making the system work and feeling that they learn or hear something from their candidate.

MR. SCHEER: If things are so rosy, how do you explain the long-run decline in participation of voters?

MR WHITE: That's what I said. This is the first step I have seen.

MR. SCHEER: One state that happened to get more attention.

MR. WHITE: That's right. I don't know whether it's going to work or not. I'm prepared to take it as an example of perhaps an increased interest and a belief that the system can be made to work, and it's the system they have got and they are going to try to work it.

What we ought to be doing, in my judgment, as both media and politicians, is dealing with people and saying okay, yes, how would you like to see us do it? Do you want the caucuses to continue? Has Iowa come up with a mix of caucus-primary like situation? Maybe they have. A lot of people participated in Iowa. That was a very good participation. Whether it was a primary or whether it was a caucus, that was good participation out there. That's a good thing. Let's listen to that, and let those of us who have a responsibility for trying to make these things function listen to that and try to make them function.

MR. GANNON: I think the Iowa experience showed that there isn't as much apathy, at least in Iowa, as is generally written about and we hear so much about. I don't think the great national malaise is out there, I doubt it isn't there last summer, but it wasn't there now. There is a sense of participation, and Iowa feels very good about what happened and I think that's good. The politicians that I have talked to in Iowa say that other caucus states have been calling and saying how did you do it, how can they make this thing work in Alaska or Minnesota, or wherever.

MR. ARTERTON: But in that sense isn't Iowa atypical? You guys sat around and deliberately made that into a big media splash with lots of attention in Iowa, brought people in there. That's not going to happen in other states.

MR. GANNON: That can be replicated, you can do that elsewhere, you can have debates, get the candidates in and talk about issues. Well, you can try. Maybe you can't.

MR. ARTERTON: What about these Florida caucuses?

MR. STEARNS: You can do it if you're first. I was going to suggest—getting to Bob Scheer's point—rather than a consolidated system of primaries, nationally or regionally, which I don't like because they're too suggestable by a sudden turn of events and we can't afford to campaign in them, it would be better to continue the process that the Winograd Commission of the Democratic Party began, which is basically trying to consolidate the process within a given period of time.

Outside of the area that the Winograd Commission set we have five states that actually hold a primary before March 11. Perhaps if we continue that process and move all states within that period so on March 11, if there are five or six other states that choose to hold a caucus or primary on that date, it's a little bit more of a challenge to campaign managers but will give the press a little more grist for the mill than simply the results of the caucuses of one state.

The Value of the Smaller Events

MR. ARTERTON: Look, the discussion of Roundtable 1 revolved around the point that wasn't it nice we have Iowas and New Hampshires where unknown candidates could go out and engage in face-to-face meetings. It seems to me we are in something of a dilemma here if this panel is now going to suggest we ought to consolidate that so that you don't go with these early small events, you're going to go with much larger increments.

MR. KRAFT: I wouldn't subscribe to that. Somebody raised that point and I thought it was a good one, that if you did have a succession of early big-state primaries—Pennsylvania, New York, Illinois—it would be a burden on an out-of-office aspirant to the presidency to get started in those states.

Obviously we like the system or the process, but I don't think it's limited to the likes of President Carter and George Bush. I think the early caucus, small-state sequence moving from either Iowa or another state like it to New England allows somebody that's not an incumbent or a national figure to run for the White House. I think that's good for the country.

MR. NAUGHTON: I wouldn't agree with national primary or any of the regional primaries. I don't get the impression the public is concerned about the process as much as it is about the consequences of it. I think there's a little bit too much tinkering with the system and rules to try to make it neater, easier for the candidates, for the press, instead of to try to get people engaged in the process and find out what's going on. I think the issues are terribly important. But we are not in a system as it now exists really coming to terms with the issues. I don't think we are grappling with that here. I don't think we are getting into the reason why the system doesn't lend itself to coming to terms with the issues except in very packaged ways. That's partly a consequence of the turn toward primaries, which tend to give you more packaging.

MR. ARTERTON: I am quite surprised here that we are talking about the vitality of caucuses, which form only about 20 percent now of the nomination process. We all agree that participation rates are lower there. We can look at the Los Angeles Times Poll and show that, where people want changes, they want changes toward more democratic processes rather than less. I assume from that that many people would see a move toward caucuses as being a move away from greater democracy.

I saw Richard Scammon take the strong point of view not a week ago that more participation is better as a *sine qua non.* The more people participate in the process, the more representative it is. We haven't talked about the representative question here, but it deserves at least some mention.

So are you really prepared to push this system back toward more caucuses? Do you think that's going to be a better way of electing a presidential candidate?

MR. NAUGHTON: The question is what does participation mean. Participation is three seconds in a booth going this way or that way. I would be for caucuses if the caucuses are going to be structured in a way that gets people involved, gets issues discussed, gets candidates poked at, nibbled at, explored, and gets some dialogue developing.

MR. KRAFT: Again, I like the mix. I don't know what the exact ratio should be between the caucus and primary states, but I think in defense of the beleaguered primary, there have been some Democratic Party reforms that have decentralized the approach the campaign has to take in a big primary state. By making a congressional district the largest unit of delegate selection that you can begin with in a large state and given the financial limitations imposed upon a campaign and the short amount of time you have in this sequence of going from Tuesday to Tuesday to Tuesday—I think you almost have to go to a primary. A primary is an expression of at least maybe 38 to 40 percent of the registered Democrats in that state, or Republicans as the case may be, and that opens it up a little. But, again, as to the ratio between caucus and primary, that's a tough one to call.

MR. STEARNS: I tend to favor the mix system much along the lines that Tim Kraft outlined. In some of the larger industrial states, caucuses have generally not been successful. Michigan's experience with caucuses in the past suggested that they are very difficult to organize on that large a scale.

More importantly, I still think with the operation of the restriction of campaign finance laws on the system, that I would rather, given the choice, have the decisions on the party's nominee made in a series of caucuses of the party than in the news rooms of the three major television networks. I think that has been the major impact of the campaign finance laws—it's really shifted power toward the news media to decide who the nominees in both parties are going to be. For that reason I would prefer to keep the mix of the caucuses and primaries.

The Importance of Being First

MR. ARTHERTON: Jim Gannon, what benefits does Iowa derive from being first? If Iowa was buried somewhere in April, would you be in favor of the Iowa caucus? Would you be able to get as much attention out there?

MR. GANNON: Clearly you wouldn't get much attention. Iowa did what it did because it was first, no question about that. I don't think it's terribly important whether you have a primary or caucus. I like the mix, too, but I don't think it matters whether you have 25 of one and 25 of the other or 40 of one and 10 of the other.

But what is important is that you somehow lure the candidates out to where that primary or caucus is and somehow get them to talk about what the people want to hear. The press can't generate issues and manufacture issues if the candidates won't talk about them. In large measure they don't want to because they don't want to take hard stands they are going to be held to later. It's very difficult to generate a debate or real engagement on the issues. The press can't manufacture that. You can try to do things in staged debates and that helps, but the candidates have to be willing to come in where the contest is and talk about what the people want to hear. If they won't do that, then the process isn't as good as it ought to be.

MR. ARTERTON: You really don't buy Tim Kraft's line that in sitting around the tables in kitchens in Iowa organizing up for the caucuses there's really good qualitative discussion of the issues?

MR. GANNON: I haven't been sitting around a lot of these tables, so I don't really know. I don't think that's the way people get their information on issues. I think we are the carriers of issue information and if the candidates will not really engage the issues, we can try all we want, but not be able to really bring them across.

MR. KRAFT: That presumes that it's the issues alone that you carry or publish that influence people to vote in the state caucuses.

MR. GANNON: People want to talk about inflation, that's supposed to be the No. 1 issue in the country. There was no talk about inflation during the Iowa caucuses; nobody mentioned it. You couldn't get Carter to talk about inflation, and nobody would listen to Kennedy talking about inflation. It was a non-issue. Yet if you look at any poll it's supposed to be the No. 1 issue in the country.

MR. KRAFT: What impels people to participate a three-hour process if it's not the issues that the Des Moines Register talks about? You talk about your candidate, your campaign, general approach and the record of your administration.

MR. GANNON: What impels them to participate is that there's a big contest going on, the world is watching, Walter Cronkite is there so it's important and we ought to do it.

MR. WHITE: It's important and also there are people that are friends involved and friends have a general attitude without a specific being involved in regard to the issue. There's a general attitude toward the issue and toward the problem, and I think that's what gets them out there to participate in the process.

MR. KRAFT: I think there's more commitment than they're given credit for.

MR. WHITE: Sure, I do, too. I think in terms of the mix—at least those of us who are alleged to be politicians here seem to favor the mix—I think what's going to happen is going to run concomitantly with how the political parties develop and survive or fail to develop and survive.

MR. ARTERTON: If there is this qualitative discussion going on in living rooms about the President's record, then it works both ways. What, Tim, did you learn from people in Iowa who were in those kitchens and living rooms that you wouldn't have known from a public opinion poll? What did you learn out of the Iowa caucuses?

MR. KRAFT: Well, I was more involved in the Iowa caucuses four years ago than I was this past time. We were in the aftermath of Watergate and some severe national stress, and people were looking for somebody with a general approach to issues and policies that they could identify with and somebody they believed in, somebody they could trust. Obviously there's a lot of focus on issues and specific issues and national problems, but I am of the belief that a large number of people in this country are motivated to vote for somebody on some vague feeling that they can confide in his judgment and not on a specific issue alone.

And I think that was prevalent in Iowa in 1976 and I think again in 1980.

Picking the Best Candidate

MR. SCHEER: I want to make one comment about our joint opportunism here. We all make a living on these things—the technicians, the campaign people, even the press—and I think we all get caught up in it much too much.

We have endless discussions of shop talk about the game. The other day, a press person said to me, "I'm not an issues person, I like the game." Much of the discussion you hear around a campaign is of that nature. There's a numbing effect to being involved in these campaigns. You're almost a square or off the wall or losing your objectivity and being consumed by passion if you dare raise an issue with some of these people; you're no longer part of the club. Other people have that perception, but I find going around these campaigns that very rarely you will hear a discussion even of whether this guy would make a good President, let alone what the issues are affecting the world or anything else.

MR. STEARNS: In a very fundamental way you're asking whether the nomination system we have as it's arranged now or been arranged for us really rewards the values that would otherwise make a person a good chief executive of the country. Maybe your ability to comprehend incomprehensible rules, to keep indefatigable schedules, contemplate 56 different events all happening on the same day are not really the sort of virtues that make you a good President.

Maybe it would be better if the Senate or Joint Chiefs of Staff picked the President. But in defense of the system, it does in the popular imagination confer on a person legitimacy to be the nominee of his party. There's some argument that it provides some kind of education of the candidate by forcing him to do a certain amount of campaigning. I would like to see the President doing more campaigning in this campaign. I assume in 1976 he got an education. I know Kennedy is getting that same education now in the course of this campaign. There may be some value in that for a person who becomes President of the United States.

Perhaps there are better systems, but given the fact this is the one we all have to work with, these are the rules provided for us, the best I can say for it is the people do accept the outcome of the system as legitimate.

MR. SCHEER: The issue is not whether you abandon the system, but whether we adopt a more self-critical attitude of our work and whether we try to do our jobs in a better way. That's the issue. I'm saying, are the press and the candidates and their aides involved in increasing the amount of hype, the amount of distortion? Or are they involved in clarifying the issues that people have to deal with? That's what I'm concerned about.

MR. STEARNS: When you talk about changes, I think the system could be consolidated more. The campaign finance laws ought to be repealed back to disclosure provisions of April of 1971. I have a lot of personal suggestions I could make about how the system in my mind might work better. But the fact is that for this election in 1980 we have got a very concrete set of rules which we are not going to change for the next few months. We are going to end up with a person who I think is legitimately the nominee of one or the other parties and someone is going to be President at the end of it.

That's what they hire us for. Yes, we're technicians. It's in the system we are given to operate with.

The Press as Adversary

MR. KRAFT: Let me further Bob Scheer's wish for self-critical analysis of both of our roles. You have not mentioned this—but it exists—there is an adversarial relationship between any campaign and a candidate and the press that covers that campaign. Frankly, the candidate feels like each speech should be crafted very carefully and each press conference response must be regarded and weighed because, with the first slip of the tongue or ill-chosen word or response, the feeling is that you will do your damndest to nail them to the wall, which you have tried to do in the past and which is part and parcel of the whole press-campaign relationship.

You talk about a meaningful discussion of the issues. I can cite numerous instances such as the energy roundtable in West Virginia in which the President and Gov. Rockefeller and Schlesinger and coal miners and mine operators and several other people sat around a table for two and a half dull numbing hours talking about the intricacies of proposed legislation and rules and regulations affecting mining in the coal industry. And the press were in the back room drinking coffee, playing cards, watching game shows and generally ignoring the damn thing because they said it was the dullest thing they had ever been subjected to. There was no controversy in the mining industry at that point that they choose to zero in on. They would rather ask a sharp question about a personality or the issue of the day that gives you the evening broadcast lead or a cute paragraph.

MR. GANNON: If the President had come out to Iowa and sat around the table for two and a half hours with a bunch of farmers and businessmen and housewives you would have gotten a hell of a lot of attention and gotten good coverage on his issues, and press wouldn't be in the back room drinking coffee. It would have been very intensively covered.

MR. KRAFT: Your point is valid. One of the most prevalent and strikingly timely issues that took place within three weeks before the caucuses was the grain embargo, and your paper covered that in extensive detail. You pointed out a remark or comment or a pledge he had made a year or two earlier about not going for an embargo and you weighed the nuances of whether his qualification of a national emergency applied at this time. Bob Bergland must have traveled to 75 or 50 small towns taking questions, going through those seminars, explaining the policy, defending the policy.

In other words, a presidential action and policy was the subject of hot and intensive debate in Iowa. And Iowans spoke. So you can't say that it was all a glib camera-oriented exercise that got them out to the caucuses. The fact was, there were some hard and sharp issues and they listened and reacted.

Summing Up

MR. ARTERTON: It seems to me we started off talking about the differences between primaries and caucuses and we quickly came to the belief that there was not much difference between them and how they would affect the system broadly. One reason for paying attention to them obviously is because they are some of the most changeable parts. We have commissions, we can change rules. We can do something. We may not be able to affect these broad things that we have been talking about in terms of whether the press will cover issues more than the horse race, whether the campaigns will talk about issues more than the nitty gritty of what's going on or give sort of flossy statements about their issues which are meant to obscure rather than to enlighten. We raised a number of questions in this session. To what extent can we deal with issues in the nominating system, primaries or caucuses. Whether the present system is satisfactory, what should be done to change it. What the role of the news media is in media events and how that's contributing to the process. We generated a situation in which the news media is, really, as Rick Stearns says, more influential in the process of our politics than our campaigns or parties. Fortunately maybe our role then is just to raise these questions because we can leave it to the next three sessions of this conference to really find solutions to these problems.

ROUNDTABLE THREE

The Impact of Television

MODERATOR

Michael S. Dukakis is a lecturer and director of intergovernmental studies at the John F. Kennedy School of Government, with responsibility for developing new programs for state and local government managers. He also teaches courses in state and local management. He was governor of Massachusetts from 1975 to 1979 and also served seven years as a Massachusetts state representative. During his term as governor, he was chairman of the National Governors Association task force on urban policy. Mr. Dukakis received his B.A. from Swarthmore College and his law degree from Harvard.

PANELISTS

Adam Clymer is a political reporter for the New York Times.

John D. Deardourff, a former aide to the late Gov. Nelson A. Rockefeller of New York, now is chairman of the board of Bailey, Deardourff and Associates. His firm coordinated advertising for the President Ford Committee in 1976 and has also assisted many congressional and gubernatorial campaigns.

Christopher Lydon is the 10 O'Clock News anchorman for WGBH-TV in Boston.

John P. Marttila is president of John Marttila and Associates, Inc. He served as consultant to the 1976 presidential campaign of Rep. Morris K. Udall and has worked with campaigns of New Jersey Gov. Brendan T. Byrne and Boston Mayor Kevin White.

Thomas Quinn is the manager of California Gov. Jerry Brown's presidential campaign and is a former chairman of the California Air Resources Board.

William J. Small is president of NBC News.

ROUNDTABLE THREE

Soaps, Shampoos and Candidates; Ideas in Small Packages; Politics as Entertainment; The 30-Second Message; A Profound Revolution; Problems With News Programming; A Real-Life Television Series; The President as Candidate; The Rising Cost of Modern Techniques; The Impact of International Crisis; Carter's Turnaround in the Polls; How Media Affect Campaigning; Taking a Stand on the Issues; A Legal Problem; Summing Up.

Soaps, Shampoos and Candidates

MICHAEL S. DUKAKIS: Let me begin by quoting something to all of you and asking you to react. This comes from an article written by Curtis Gans which appeared back in the spring of 1979. Gans writes the following, "This is an argument for an idea whose time has not yet come. It is, however, an idea whose time had better come soon for the health and welfare of American democracy.

"For if there is one legislative remedy that might reverse the growing and pervasive American distrust with politics and the increasing desertion of Americans from the polling booth, it is this, abolish the paid political television commercial.

"Abolish the marching drummers, swinging to the tune of I'm feeling good about America. Eliminate the fast-paced clips of the strong man with his shirt sleeves rolled up, his tie at half-mast, jacket slung over his shoulder, and his jaw set in his determination to tackle the second toughest job in America.

"Blow away the radioactive mushroom-shaped cloud hovering over the little girl picking daisies or the rooster-shaped weather vane whose 180-degree swings meter the candidate's expressed view. Cancel the star-studded galas and send the glamorous back to Hollywood to endorse the soaps and shampoos, their experience with which may make them qualified to serve as judges for the rest of us."

Well, that's Curtis Gans in the spring of 1979. Assuming that there is no constitutional problem with this proposal—obviously we all know that there might be and probably is—what do you think about it? Should we abolish the paid political television commercial?

John, since your economic fortune might rest on this.

JOHN D. DEARDOURFF: I concede a conflict of interest. Let me just say very bluntly that I think at least in that statement Curtis Gans' rhetoric has outrun his intellect. I am personally convinced that the abolishing of paid political advertising would be an enormous disservice to the political process and that it ought to be rejected out of hand. If you look at television, first of all, for what it is, it is clearly the most powerful communications tool that has ever been devised. If you go beyond that and ask yourself in what way is television available to the political candidate, it seems to me you only have three options available.

First of all, there is the availability of the news. There is the availability of so-called talk shows, which are a form of news, but increasingly an unreliable form in my judgment where you have paid newsmen interviewing candidates. Or you have paid advertising. Those are the only three options that a candidate has in order to communicate through television to mass audiences.

My own view is that paid advertising is the most reliable, the most effective, and the only one of those three vehicles in which a candidate is able to say exactly what he or she wants to say in the words that he or she wants to use with a certainty of the delivery of the precise message that the candidate wants to deliver.

Now, how the campaign chooses to use that time is another question and a much larger and more important question to me. But to remedy whatever deficiencies there are in the use of television advertising by outlawing its use seems to me to be just fundamentally incorrect. There are serious questions about the lengths of availabilities over which we have no control, incidentally. I mean frequently I hear criticisms of the 30-second commercial.

MR. DUKAKIS: By length of availabilities, what do you mean?

Ideas in Small Packages

MR. DEARDOURFF: I'm talking of the length of time a candidate is able to purchase from the networks or from the local stations. We are, in effect, in terms of buying advertising, forced into certain time frames—30 seconds, one minute, occasionally five minutes, rarely anything longer than that.

My own view is that is an artificial constriction that I would prefer to avoid, but I also do not happen to believe that you can't say something quite important in 30 seconds or less. In fact, I think one of the great myths of television advertising is that it is impossible to communicate effectively in less than some predetermined length. I could tell voters all they might want to know about a candidate's position on any issue in 30 seconds or less if I choose to do that.

MR. DUKAKIS: Frightening statement. (Laughter) Maybe you're right.

CHRISTOPHER LYDON: Maybe you could tell people everything he knew about it. (Laughter)

MR. DUKAKIS: Is there anybody around the table that wants to defend Gans or at least explain to us why he's got this concern?

ADAM CLYMER: What about the idea of not banning the commercial, not banning the candidate saying what he wants to say, but of—since we have skipped over the First Amendment problem—requiring a certain amount of time to be available for the candidate to come in and say something to the camera. Get rid of the Tinker Toys, get rid of the Joe Garagiolas and the songs, but yes, let Howard Baker or Jerry Brown or even Jimmy Carter come out and say what he thinks about something, let him attack the guy he's running against or tell about his family or whatever it is he thinks makes him qualified to be President. While it may be possible to communicate ideas in 30-second spots, I have a feeling that the ideas that are communicated that way are kind of sleazy.

MR. DUKAKIS: What about that? Mal McDougall, an advertising man who was deeply involved in the advertising for Jerry Ford's campaign in 1976, said he wouldn't abolish the paid political commercial, but he'd require the person buying the time to appear in at least two-thirds of that 30 seconds or minute or two or five and actually speak to people rather than simply have one of these hoked-up things.

THOMAS QUINN: There's not a mystery as to who the person is. I don't understand Adam Clymer's point. In a presidential campaign, people know who the candidates are, they know what they look like. I don't think there's any deception taking place. Gov. Brown this year has commercials similar to what Adam describes. He's sitting there, looking right at the camera, giving his message. But I think if somebody else wants to do it differently, I don't see deception, any problem there.

MR. DUKAKIS: He said it's sleazy. It bothers him, and I gather it bothers him because of its impact on the process.

MR. QUINN: Is it more sleazy than a candidate going out to do some kind of a stunt so the network TV cameras will go out and cover that stunt?

MR. CLYMER: No, just about as sleazy.

MR. QUINN: I remember in 1970 when John Tunney was running for Senate in California, he went on a dive in the Santa Barbara Channel with all of his diving outfit down there and apparently almost drowned. The whole idea was to dramatize his position against offshore oil drilling in the channel. I guess if he wants to do that and cameras want to cover that, that's legitimate. I don't see how you can censor that any more than we can censor what the New York Times prints about a campaign.

MR. CLYMER: I don't think we want to censor it. We sort of put the First Amendment problems for all of these restrictions aside for the sake of argument as to what would be a useful thing. But I would rather hear Gov. Brown for five minutes than for 30 seconds, because I think the amount of an idea that you can communicate in 30 seconds is the vaguest taste of one, and I think it leads candidates and campaigns to oversimplify even more than they would otherwise.

MR. QUINN: That's a different issue. That's the issue John Deardourff raised, the issue of time availability. And you cannot buy to my knowledge on any station, almost any station in the country, anything longer than 30 seconds during prime-time evening hours.

MR. DURAKIS: I don't think that's what's bothering Gans or even Adam Clymer when he talks about sleaziness. It seems to me what is being expressed is a kind of vague feeling of unease about methods of trying to huckster a candidate, which in the opinion of a lot of people have some very serious implications for the way we pick our presidents.

Politics as Entertainment

MR. LYDON: There's everything wrong with Gans' definition, although he frames it interestingly. First of all, you cannot suspend the First Amendment. In a profound way that's what he wants to do. He wants to repeal the most effective means of publication, of expression. And you simply cannot do it. The print media cannot repeal it. That's a print mentality trying to repeal the electronic mentality. You just can't do it.

Furthermore, the problem is not the paid commercial. Politics now takes place on unpaid television, in news, and particularly in the presidential thing on these Tuesday night winter early primaries and caucuses which we have seen dramatically in Iowa already. But television is now the medium of politics as entertainment series, as a sort of real-life thriller series that in 1976 dramatically took place. It was a 10 o'clock Tuesday night series. That was when Cronkite and the others came in and gave us essentially what became the adventures of little Jimmy Carter—watch Jimmy run, watch Jimmy improve, watch Jimmy surprise us again. And it seems to me the Carter campaign essentially grew and was the model for the Bush campaign and others this year as a process of introducing of a bit player, the way I think John Travolta emerged in Welcome Back Kotter. (Laughter)

You introduce a character. You hope to have your man in that spot in this conflict series, this real-life public conflict, in which the public and the political world will say, hey, that's good, strengthen that character, double his part, bring him forward, make him a star.

I think the whole problem with commercials is sort of historical. I don't think that's really where George Bush or Jimmy Carter or Ronald Reagan or John Connally or anybody really thinks of emerging. The game now is to strike a much subtler resonance with the country's appetite for drama, and you sell it Tuesday nights on unpaid time and then you amplify it, if you're successful, with paid commercials. In other words, there's a sort of obsolescence of that question because television has moved well beyond that. In 1980 the real problem for Carter was to figure out how do we really keep the drama going over a 13-week, coincidentally a 13-week period, from the first primary to the crucial ones. But that is a television series length. It is a process of sustaining a drama, not wearing it out too fast, not bringing it on too soon, bringing it on with all the family complexity, with all the personality sort of interest that television series require, and sustaining it over that 13-week bridge.

That all sounds a little crazy, I think, a little cynical. I don't mean it humorously, though, but I also would like to refocus peoples' attention on the possibility at least that that is really what television is doing to this campaign. The problem is not the commercial.

MR. DUKAKIS: It's something else. Bill Small, you're in the business of running a major national news system and operation. A television model of presidential campaigns—is that what we are doing, a 13-week series?

WILLIAM J. SMALL: Let me make some brief observations. Tom Quinn is oversimplifying the question of commercial time. It is not true that you're limited to 30 seconds. You may be limited by other factors, but just last Sunday night, Lyndon LaRouche, who hardly has the kind of resources that major party candidates have, was on a network for half an hour.

MR. QUINN: How many half-hours will the networks sell him?

MR. SMALL: It depends. With the current atmosphere at the FCC we may all be in a posture where all we will be seeing are half-hour political broadcasts because they have been ruling in favor of candidates in terms of paid commercial time.

The 30-Second Message

MR. QUINN: What's the policy right now?

MR. SMALL: Something that John Deardourff said at the very start intrigued me and I want to pose the question and get back to this. Could you give us an example of a 30-second commercial that tells everything a candidate wants to say about the subject?

MR. DEARDOURFF: Sure. As a matter of fact, I just wrote one. (Laughter)

MR. SMALL: And it only took 30 seconds to write.

MR. DEARDOURFF: Let me just say that I really think that it is a very unfortunate simplification to believe that one cannot say as much as the overwhelming majority of voters want or need to know about a subject in that length of time. We are not talking about pleasing Adam Clymer and the readers of the New York Times when we are communicating on television. He has a market for what he writes and obviously he writes at great length about what interests him and interests his readers.

We are talking about many millions of people whose level of interests, whose level of education, whose level of intensity about any politician or a political campaign is much removed from that of the typical reader of the Los Angeles Times or the New York Times or any other major newspaper in this country. And the problem of the political communicator, the candidate and his staff, is to somehow communicate effectively. By effective communication I mean communication that influences the vote of that viewer. That's what a political campaign is about. It's not to amuse or enlighten the press as much as it is to communicate effectively to the voter.

But to get back to my 30-second commercial, the subject is abortion. And my position is as follows: I believe that the question of abortion is one that ought to be reserved exclusively to a woman and her doctor. I favor giving women the unfettered right to abortion. I also favor the federal funding of abortions through Medicaid for poor women as an extension of that right to an abortion and I oppose any statutory or constitutional limitations on that right. That's 24 seconds. I don't know how much more one needs to know about that subject in order to form an opinion if that's an issue about which you're concerned.

JOHN P. MARTTILA: It's important to understand why campaigns gravitate toward a 30-second commercial. What John said at the outset is very important. Television is the most effective form of political communication, and 30-second commercials are available during prime-time television between the hours of 7:30 and the 11 o'clock news. That is when the vast majority of the American people watch television.

The time that Bill Small spoke about is generally made available during lesser times. In fact in 1976, I believe, one or two of the presidential campaigns sued the networks to buy five-minute time for fund-raising purposes during prime time, and I think it was Frank Church's campaign that did that and finally succeeded.

MR. SMALL: For the record, LaRouche was on 10:30 to 11 on Sunday night, prime time.

MR. MARTTILA: Most strategists recognize—unfortunately and with some benefits—that 30-second television is, for lack of a better way to look at it, the battleground of a campaign as far as media is concerned. If you want to reach the most people, 30-second TV is what campaigns need. Normally between 7:30 and 11 o'clock you cannot buy one-minute, two-minute, five-minute television, a serious problem. Campaigns have to deal with that as a political reality, they have to solve it, and that means 30-second television.

Going back to Gans' opening remarks, I believe, focusing on 30-second TV alone is hardly an answer. We have to look at the entire process, and what's happened in the 1970s is that American politics have gone through a profound change. It does not resemble the politics of the 1960s. There is much more money, much more media, much more survey research. It's a much more media-oriented kind of politics and much less people-intensive kind of politics. Any appropriate reform would have to deal with the entire environment rather than just the 30-second commercials.

A Profound Revolution

MR. DUKAKIS: If what you say, John, is accurate, and that is there has been a profound revolution and the media and particularly the electronic media have a lot to do with it, are our presidential campaigns now basically a situation comedy or 13-week series or whatever you want to call it? Is that really the way we are doing this? Is that an accurate perception for one? And secondly, is that a good thing for the American political system in the selection of presidents?

MR. MARTTILA: I don't subscribe. There are people of good will inside most of the presidential campaigns I have known. They care about the issues deeply, they work very hard, and I think they try to structure their campaigns to be politically effective, and there is a level of idealism. But the fundamental point is that television has changed American life, and I don't think we still fully understand or even begin to understand how profound the change is. Right now the average American family watches three and a half hours of television per day. That's an extraordinary statistic. The implications of that for their participation in civic affairs—school, religious events and so forth—I think is quite staggering. It obviously has had an impact on the political process.

MR. DUKAKIS: Has it had the impact Chris Lydon thinks it has?

MR. LYDON: No question of good intentions or idealism or anything else. I was simply trying to describe—and I think accurately—where the essential forum of presidential politics is now, and it's a prime-time, unpaid news series format on an intense weekly production through the late winter months. Of course there are idealists as well as con men and flim-flammers and everything else. They have always been involved. I'm just saying this is where it takes place. But to go back a step and clarify a point, does anybody think in this rather extraordinary campaign we have already with Carter down and up and Reagan and the whole bit—does anybody think that the 30-second spot or any of those other questions that we have been talking about have been important? I don't think we do. I don't think anybody feels that the girl with the daisy and the bomb (a 1964 commercial) or any of those questions have really been important in what we have seen so far.

I think the commercial thing is a dead question.

MR. QUINN: We began on the wrong track here. The issue is 30 minutes, not 30 seconds. It's the 30-minute network television newscast every night.

I think we would be better off examining the implications of that.

MR. DUKAKIS: We are going to go to that. But let me stay with this for just a second. Do you all agree that paid political advertising is something that really is no longer important? I assume, John Deardourff, you think it's important because you're advising candidates and clients all the time to spend money on it.

MR. CLYMER: I think one of the reasons it's important is the point Tom is trying to get at; that is, that this is one way of getting a message across when the news shows or the availability of longer periods of time are not as satisfactory as some of the candidates think they ought to be or may be. If you can't get a message through that way, then you need John's 24 seconds.

MR. DUKAKIS: He would tell you it's a very important part of the way you get your message across.

Problems with News Programming

MR. DEARDOURFF: Absolutely. It is the only reliable way in which a candidate can communicate directly to the voters. Without being critical necessarily of news programming or talk shows or anything else, that is a filter between the candidate and the voters. It's at sort of a fundamental level here—you're talking about what television is. Is it a conduit to be used by people who want to communicate with other people directly, or is it a filtering process by which the views of people, whether political candidates or others, are filtered through some apparatus controlled by the ownership of these television stations and then distributed?

The problem I have with news programming or talk shows or anything else is that, from the point of view of the candidate, they are simply unreliable. They are not predictable in terms of our need to communicate directly. They are a filter, not a conduit.

MR. MARTTILA: I'd like to ask John Deardourff about his interpretation of the role of paid advertising in the Iowa caucuses. How influential do you think it was?

MR. DEARDOURFF: I think it was of some significance. One of the questions we ought to address—although I don't know the answer—is that of measuring the impacts of various types of communication. In Iowa you had a saturation not only of paid advertising, but also of news coverage. And there is no way that I know of to filter out the impact of television versus the other ways in which people are observing the campaigns. It is fair to say that in the case of Sen. Baker, with whom we are working, it was significant. I think it was significant in a larger sense in expanding public interest in that campaign.

Now, I don't claim that that was the sole result of paid advertising. I think there were lots of other things. But it is interesting, at least, that with this substantial increase in advertising in Iowa, you also got a very substantial quantum jump in turnout. And I think that is a positive effect of television. There is an argument being made in some scholarly journals that the effect of television advertising and television in general is to drive down the voter turnout. I don't think that's true at all.

MR. DUKAKIS: It certainly didn't happen in Iowa. Christopher Lydon, what do you think about all of this? These fellows say if they were advising clients—they are, candidates today—they would tell them to put a substantial amount of money into paid political advertising.

MR. LYDON: Of course, just the same way you'd put money into organization and phone banks and newspaper advertising and other things. Television probably is more important. With all due respect to John Deardourff, I think Baker was not the story of the Iowa caucuses. The story of the Iowa caucuses had nothing to do with paid political advertising. It was the dramatic recasting of Jimmy Carter as a wholly new kind of figure which was done largely by events externally and largely by his understanding of what he had to do with them. It was done by this almost still unexplained collapse—it may be only temporary—of Ted Kennedy's morale and of his support, and it was the story of George Bush's emergence in what I think is the new model or the current model of the way candidates succeed. Again, none of the big events so far have been the product, good or bad, of the paid commercial.

MR. CLYMER: There's a Carter commercial which underlined the whole thing you're talking about, which said in essence, show the Russians, vote Carter. That was an awfully strong and effective commercial which affected this point you're talking about.

MR. SMALL: Chris, you cannot dismiss what television did for Baker. Baker came out of Iowa viable and respectable and alive; Dole did not.

MR. LYDON: The finger pointing, the commercial, I grant you.

MR. SMALL: Okay, but that's the point, that the television commercial saved a candidate who came in late with poorer organization than the others. It did have an impact.

MR. LYDON: Of course it did, I'm not denying that. I think we are not yet focusing on the big game.

MR. DUKAKIS: Let me interrupt and ask a couple of rather pointed questions. The Carter rebirth—aided perhaps by paid commercials and effective organization—has had a great deal to do with certain major international events, the fact that he's the President and the fact that the public as a whole is rallying around him and conceivably thinks he's been handling them reasonably well under the circumstances.

The Bush arrival on the scene strikes me as being an example of good, hard, old-fashioned, grass-roots organization. Now, it may very well be that television has helped to amplify or expand on these forces, but then you get underneath that and it sounds to me as if it's the same old business.

I say that in a very positive way—external events, the President in the White House handling them, the relatively unknown candidate who goes out and organizes the grass roots. Isn't that American politics pretty much the way we have understood it? Or am I missing something?

MR. LYDON: I don't think so, no. George Bush's wisdom was realizing, as John Connally didn't and Reagan didn't, that that was the whole game, was to go to those caucuses, forgetting other states, because networks were going to move millions of dollars of talent and equipment and sets, and the whole bit, to Iowa to make a phenomenal amplification of that, not a little amplification. Think back to 1960. John Kennedy did a lot of that Wisconsin stuff by himself, nobody there, no reporters—nothing. Word very slowly drifted back.

MR. DUKAKIS: Some may disagree with you. I think Kennedy's victory in the West Virginia primary was one of the most important single events in the 1960 presidential campaign.

A Real-Life Television Series

MR. LYDON: But the speed with which those little victories are amplified now I think is wholly different. Let me give you a quick history in terms of my metaphor of the Carter fall and the Carter rebirth, going back to the Carter birth.

It seems to me when you look back at Carter, whom I covered a lot of for the New York Times and even then I thought that what Carter did in Iowa was classic manipulation, maybe luck, but maybe manipulation, too, of those amplifying qualities of the early primaries.

One thing he realized was that an event in Iowa took place in living rooms all over the country all at the same time. Looking back, it seems to me he appealed in Iowa almost exclusively as a television character. He was peanut farmer with the teeth, with the wrinkled lovable mother, with the 13-year-old daughter, whatever she was then, the family, this sort of Bible-thumping Annapolis engineer. He was a good television character. But he also was a very weak political character, and the thing that got me thinking about all this was that I was always struck by how politically empty Jimmy Carter was in terms of an issue, in terms of even organizing or organizational kinds of people, in terms of a constituency.

Jimmy Carter succeeded all this time the way a television character grabs dramatic interest—what's he doing, good, he's doing so much better than we thought. He had an excitement, and George Bush again is repeating the same thing. George Bush doesn't say he's got anything except momentum. The whole game now is to get rating points. Rating points generate rating points. In any case, Carter in my view got into the White House without a block constituency, without an organizing issue, without a friendly network of pols around the country. But he had television presence. Like all television characters, it wore out. I was already thinking on these lines maybe a year into the Carter presidency when things were beginning to fall apart and Russell Baker, whom I always take seriously, began a column saying that, if Jimmy Carter were a TV series, he would have been canceled by now.

I thought aha, he's onto it, too. That's what the game is about, and as Carter went down and down and down in the polls, I kept saying to myself, he hasn't done anything wrong, we are not in war, there's no depression yet, he's not a thief.

Jimmy Carter's great failure in his down time was that he got boring. The family got worn out. Billy was a bore, Miss Lillian was a bore. (Laughter and applause) The kids had moved into the White House, had moved out, you couldn't ever move them in again. Amy—the characters were exhausted, peanut farmer, you just try something else. Try another series.

We are stuck with a four-year constitutional term, so what do you do? The reason I thought Carter couldn't come back was that you couldn't recycle those characters. But he did. He came up with Jimmy as commander in chief, Jimmy as general, Jimmy the war president. And it's going like gangbusters. We have a new series on our hands.

MR. DUKAKIS: This is a very intriguing view of the world. Tom Quinn, you're in it, you're managing a presidential campaign. Is this what it's all about?

MR. QUINN: I think what Chris Lydon says is so obvious as to be irrefutable when you look at what happened to Gerald Ford, who wasn't quite as good a performer or maybe he didn't have as good direction as Jimmy Carter may have. When the Pueblo was captured, we had more people than we have in our embassy in Iran, and they were held hostage much longer than the situation has gone on in Iran so far. But we didn't have network TV crews over there every night telling us what had happened. We didn't have demonstrators out there—because there were TV crews—demonstrating, holdings signs, yelling kill Carter, kill America. We didn't have the show going on. So we didn't have the inflamed passions here in America.

MR. DUKAKIS: I was seven in 1940 when Wendell Wilkie was challenging Franklin Roosevelt for the presidency and there was a very serious question in this country of whether a President ought to serve more than two terms. The most telling argument as I recall was that we were on the verge of international cataclysm, that this man was in charge and had been the commander in chief for eight years. You didn't want to change in the middle of the stream at that time.

MR. QUINN: I suggest there's a different situation here. We have not been on the verge of war, we don't have Adolf Hitler marching through Europe already.

MR. SMALL: I'm not sure everyone would be as comfortable with that conclusion.

MR. QUINN: I suggest we have an incumbent President who wants to be reelected, as he should want to be reelected, and who is playing a pretty dangerous game of deliberately trying to inflame the passions so he can have a new TV series.

The President as Candidate

MR. CLYMER: One thing that does make it somewhat different than 1940 is the topic of our panel, television. Yes, the same arguments were there, but the impact, the domination of the evening news by the Iran story, the way that evening television news—as John Deardourff's client, Gerald Ford, was able to demonstrate four years ago—will fall for the silliest gimmick of a picture of a President. It dramatizes the rescue of those six hostages to show on television the fact that the President of United States talks on the phone to the prime minister of Canada.

The ability of the networks to fall for the Rose Garden strategy in one form or another, that magnifies those effects, and I think it may magnify them to the degree that it makes a difference. Take a look at the questions of the way the networks deal with these things. The Republican debate in Iowa was a legitimate news event considered worth covering by the television networks, not maybe enthusiastically, as long as there was a Democratic debate. The President pulls out of the Democratic debate, and whatever that does to the fortunes of Mr. Quinn's candidate (Gov. Brown), and Sen. Kennedy, the Republican debate was there just the way it had been. One of the networks said Reagan isn't going to be there, so we won't cover it. Reagan had never said he would be there. They copped out on that one quickly.

That is the kind of thing that accentuates the sort of element that Tom Quinn and the Kennedy campaign in particular and to some degree the Republican candidates now are very unhappy about, this tremendous focus on the President. The failure of the networks is to figure out any way of coping with one candidate who is campaigning and the other one is just being presidential. They cover Kennedy with little jabs. CBS the other night went so far as to say, he then turned to his TelePrompTer and read. The fellow who introduced Phil Jones to do that spot was Walter Cronkite and it seems to me that he uses that same device.

All right, this is a bit of cuteness that television uses because in 30 or 60 or 90 seconds you can't get too deep in your discussion, so you show you're not being fooled, you show you're being balanced by these little jabs. If only one candidate is out campaigning, he's the only candidate to get jabbed. I don't think they think about it.

MR. DUKAKIS: I still want to get into this very fundamental question here. John Marttila said we were in the middle of the communications revolution. TV has had an enormous impact on society and in particular on how we campaign and pick our presidents. Chris Lydon has elaborated on that in a very interesting way and thinks it's absolutely central to what's going on these days. What about that? I mean is it really that or isn't it pretty much the same business with a little gloss, but with many of the same considerations making the difference, when we pick our presidents?

The Rising Cost of Modern Techniques

MR. MARTTILA: Let me give you some statistics which might put this in perspective. I think first of all we are blending separable issues—first the impact of paid television commercials on presidential campaigns and second the network coverage. I submit that the impact of the paid television commercial will still make itself felt before it is over, most notably within the Republican primary just as it did in 1976 within the Democratic primary. I think the two or three candidates who really focused most of their energies on mastering paid television commercials were the ones who ultimately were the most successful. President Carter, Mo Udall and Scoop Jackson, at the outset of his campaign, spent most of their efforts on that part of the campaign.

But let me tell you about American politics. In 1978 the total cost for all the congressional and Senate campaigns in the United States was $194 million. By way of contrast, the parliamentary elections in Great Britain were $3 million. In 1976 the average cost of a Senate campaign in the United States was $600,000. In 1978 the average cost was $920,000. There is just a whole new rapid growth of huge infusions of money, and it's a cliche that most analysts understand that most of that money is being spent on television. I think intelligent campaigns spend between 65 and 70 percent of their money, and some campaign resources, on media-related activities. These statistics and the win/loss ratios behind these statistics document the enormous influence of paid television advertising within our political system. I think it had a direct bearing on the outcome of the 1976 Democratic primary and it will have an effect in 1980.

MR. CLYMER: A lot of the difference in expenditures is because the same 30 seconds cost substantially more.

MR. MARTTILA: Congressional Reports has done an analysis of that. The increased costs of campaigning are 35 to 40 percent over the inflationary rates of the past years.

MR. DUKAKIS: Assuming that candidates believe it's effective, what effect does that have on how we pick our presidents? Does it mean that, as a result of these enormous financial burdens brought on by the cost of television advertising, we are turning candidates over into the hands of special interests? Or are there some implications for this? Carter was the guy that started out without an awful lot of money, kind of a poor man, small-town candidate, and made it. Are there some serious implications in terms of how we pick our presidents?

MR. MARTTILA: I think there are. In spite of what I have been saying, I think we need to seriously reform our presidential politics.

MR. DUKAKIS: In what way? Based on the impact of the cost of television?

MR. MARTTILA: If you look at the results of this new trend, I think you can see three or four very disturbing signs. First of all, in 1960, which was a presidential campaign, 62 percent of the American public voted. In 1976 it was only 37 percent. It's been a straight downhill erosion. Whatever is happening to American society right now, participation is decreasing.

MR. DUKAKIS: Do you blame television for that?

MR. MARTTILA: It's part of the entire mix. To focus only on 30-second commercials or just the network news coverage or just the impact of survey research is a mistake. We have to stand back and look at the entire process. The real foundations of modern campaigning are survey research and television and their ability to really direct and control the conduct of a campaign, at least the paid resources. I think this is having quite a profound effect.

The diminishing of our party structure has lessening importance today. Most candidates around the country circumvent the local party organization. There is more now in presidential politics. There's a whole series of issues that have to be looked at here.

MR. DUKAKIS: Can we look at those? They are really very profound. John Marttila has laid out at least three critical impacts that he says the arrival of television had on the way we pick presidential candidates. One, it costs a heck of a lot of money. Second, he thinks or suspects television is having the effect of reducing public participation in campaigns. And third, he thinks it's doing a job on the party structure. What about that? Start with financial burdens. Is that what's happening, Tom Quinn, and if so, is it a good or bad thing?

MR. QUINN: Obviously it costs a lot of money.

MR. DUKAKIS: Are you troubled by that?

MR. QUINN: I'm troubled that I can't raise it, yes. But that's not what troubles me most. I hope we sometime get around to it. I'd like to get back to Chris Lydon's point later on. Raising money is a serious problem. You have to spend most of your money on television. If you look in this morning's paper at what the various candidates have spent to date, you'll find that most of them have spent what they have raised, whether it be $2 million or $4 million. But that money has not been spent, at least not very significantly, on TV advertising.

MR. SMALL: So far.

MR QUINN: So far. It's been spent on other kinds of politicking. That means people out there running this year have spent two million, three million, four million dollars basically without yet going on television. They have done that before the very first primary. When you look at the cost of television, you somehow have to take into account the fact there must be something else that costs a lot of money—traveling in jet airplanes. The escalation in air fares is a serious problem for our campaign. All the campaigns find it costs a lot more to get around right now. So TV becomes a burden in terms of cost a little bit later in the primary season as you get on to the Florida primaries, get on to Illinois, particularly, then New York State, eventually out to Ohio, California, those big states.

MR. SMALL: New York, Ohio, California will not be problems because I have been calculating 13 weeks will be up.

MR. QUINN: That was the beginning.

MR. LYDON: I think money is a phony issue. The country spends vastly more money figuring out what's the best football team in America every year than we spend picking a president. It's peanuts in a rich country like this. I think there ought to be lots more money in it. You'd involve lots more people if you took the lid off spending, and you'd get back some of the investment.

MR. QUINN: It becomes more difficult because of the reform laws. We saw in the election four years ago that candidates didn't have buttons, didn't have bumper strips, didn't want volunteers around. Later on in the latter part of the general election campaign out at the Carter headquarters in Los Angeles, we had to discourage people. We couldn't afford to print literature and give out buttons and bumper stickers. That money had to go for other purposes, primarily television in that case. It would have been easy to raise money for Ford and Carter, but there's a prohibition on that. The money problem probably relates more to the legal limitations. I think there was a serious error in thinking in the drafting of the reform law. There should have been an overall limit on spending and not a limit on contributions.

I don't think that is the key problem for us. I do think there is a serious problem that exists within the format of television news coverage of campaigns, and I don't think that's the fault of the people working in TV news. Bill Small has 30 minutes to fill up, minus commercials that's 24 or something, and I think I've heard it compared to four columns of the front page of the New York Times. There just isn't that much time. That's not very much news to put on the air every night on NBC Nightly News. They have to make judgments. And when you have an overriding international event such as we have been seeing these last few months, those events take up a lot of time. We had weeks going by when I'm certain more than half of the network newscasts were being devoted to one event, and that one event was being directed in many ways by the commander in chief as you would expect in times of tension and war.

The Impact of International Crisis

MR. DUKAKIS: That's the nature of the business. He is the President, he is an incumbent. At a time of crisis the incumbent, if he's handling it reasonably well, tends to benefit. Has television made this any different?

MR. QUINN: I think so. It is different. I think it created image. My little boy is 12 years old. I remember sitting on Thanksgiving, at my mother's house, and he went upstairs to watch TV news. There were a bunch of people in Iran, burning American flags and holding up signs saying kill Americans so on. My 12-year-old—we try to have a peaceful family—says bomb them, bomb them, bomb them. Very emotional. I said, calm down a second. He said no, let's bomb them, why don't we drop the H-bomb. I'm not trying to universalize the reaction of a 12-year-old, but I think there was a hysteria created, an impression somehow or other that a cataclysmic event was happening, and it was happening every night. I think that affected what happened in the New York Times. It became such a massive event I think the print press probably covered it more than they might have and treated it a little bit differently.

To this day I don't think, at least on television, there has been background coverage. Papers like the New York Times and Washington Post have covered other aspects—how did we get into Iran, how did all of this happen, why was the Shah admitted, why was the doctor selected. A lot of things that aren't relevant to today have been printed in the print press, but they haven't been examined on television.

MR. SMALL: That's nonsense, Tom. There have been more specials on Iran.

MR. QUINN: ABC gives us five nights a week America Held Hostage, but the basic questions as to how we got there have not been examined. (Applause)

MR. SMALL: If you watch the specials on all three commercial networks as well as PBS, you will find that there are more in-depth treatments of how we got there. If you go back and examine the schedules of all four networks—PBS and three commercial networks—you'll find, ABC's 11:30 specials aside, more special broadcasts devoted to this subject than any similar subject in my memory. It is not just on evening news and these broadcasts. CBS in the last week alone did a five-part series, the second of which was devoted entirely to the nature of the Islamic community, if you will, and how it relates to this issue. So I don't believe that what you're saying is true at all.

MR. QUINN: I think you're supporting my point and agreeing with me.

MR. SMALL: I'm only addressing myself to the point you make about background and interpretation of events.

MR.QUINN: I wasn't clear then on what I meant.

MR. SMALL: All right. If you're talking about Iran and then Iran and Afghanistan and then Iran and the Olympics, dominating the news picture, it is true—true on television, true in print. But as Gov. Dukakis suggests, that has always been the case. If a Pueblo situation arises, that will dominate the news. I'm sorry that Jerry Brown cannot be the lead story on a network newscast as often as you'd like, but there are other things happening in this world.

MR. QUINN: I'm trying to point out that we have had other crises, recent crises. We went through Vietnam. That was a war where we were killing people, we were being killed, we had soldiers being killed, and we didn't have the same kind of intensity day in and day out in terms of the specials—ABC is a good example every night—that we are having now.

MR. SMALL: I can just tell you that every question you have raised has been done on all three networks time and again.

MR. QUINN: I don't think so.

MR. DUKAKIS: I want to get back to the impact of all of this on how we pick our presidents and whether or not television as such has made a radical, major, dramatic change in the way we do that.

MR. LYDON: We all agree it has.

MR. DUKAKIS: I'm not sure I'm persuaded. I can keep quoting history to you. I mean the Rose Garden, Warren Harding on the front porch. Is it so much different, has television made the difference?

MR. LYDON: It's immensely different. We know the party structure has no meaning.

MR. DUKAKIS: Get into that for a second. I remember a party structure back in the 1930s and 1940s and 1950s in which southern Democrats voted regularly with Republicans, in which everybody bemoaned the lack of party responsibility, the lack of clear ideological lines between the parties—and what did the parties stand for at that time? Nobody could quite tell. Has there been a major change and has television done that to us?

Carter's Turnaround in the Polls

MR. LYDON: Franklin Roosevelt was not at 19 percent (as Carter was in the ABC News-Haris poll on his ability to handle the nation's energy problems). I'm sort of amazed at how much better Carter understands the process than we do, all of us at this table.

I don't discount the possibility, I really don't, that one day when Hamilton Jordan writes his ultimate memoir, that there will have been a meeting about letting the Shah in and Jimmy says, geez, Hamilton, you know, the State Department tells me right here there will be hell to pay, that the embassy isn't secure. Hamilton says, I told the President, Mr. President, you're going right nowhere as is.

MR. DUKAKIS: Let's do everything we can to make it possible for the hostages to be seized. Are you seriously susggesting that?

MR. LYDON: Of course, I am, Michael, how do you think he became President?

MR. DEARDOURFF: Come on, really.

MR. LYDON: What we do know is that Jimmy Carter was at 19 in the polls and going down, that the Shah wanted to come in.

MR. CLYMER: He was coming back up by the beginning of November.

MR. MARTTILA: George Gallup described Carter's reversal in the polls as the most extraordinary political rebirth in the history of his 40 years in polling, and I think it's important to deal with the Carter renaissance as possibly one specific situation which kind of defies the normal rule of political recovery.

MR. LYDON: So do I. But if Jimmy Carter understands television as I think he does, it would be utterly plausible on the basis of everything we know. Essentially these things happened: he was being creamed by Kennedy in the polls . . . The other thing we forget when we talk about things having changed—Roosevelt had a congressional program, he had dealt with a tremendous economic crisis, he had built a mighty constituency in this country north and south in different ways.

Jimmy Carter had done none of those things. He was going nowhere in the polls. The State Department warns him that there will be hell to pay in Tehran and that the embassy is not secure, but that the Shah needs medical treatment in New York. Jimmy knows you can get medical treatment elsewhere. But he goes right ahead and does that thing that he is warned will have a specific effect, and it does. We may not like to talk about it, but Hamilton knows that when it hits the fan abroad, there's only one commander in chief and everything that has happened since then, it seems to me, was anticipatable by a guy as smart as Hamilton. I think we are sort of kidding ourselves that they wouldn't do that sort of thing with the Oval Office.

MR. SMALL: If they were so good at television, how did he get down to 19 percent in the first place? (Laughter and applause)

MR. LYDON: You know how series wear out; a lot of great series wear out.

MR. DUKAKIS: John Deardourff has been remarkably restrained.

MR. DEARDOURFF: Carter's standing in the polls—early, late, today—bears a direct relationship to the reality that's going on in the world. It's not that he is such an effective manipulator of events. When the public was focused on the fact that inflation was up and unemployment was up and interest rates were up and there was a failure across the board in policy, he was down. At a time now when he appears to be handling certain events reasonably well, he's up. And that he's up and down is also relative in terms of his competition. So that I just must say it's a fascinating notion of Chris', but I think wrong.

MR. SMALL: John, if you were handling Carter right now, how secure would you feel with that stand?

MR. DEARDOURFF: That's the point I wanted to make. There is a difference today, and the difference that television makes is in the immediacy of events all over the world, and that immediacy in turn means very quick fluctuations in public sentiment about a whole range of events. In 1940 or in 1950 or even in 1960 you could not have changed public opinion on these subjects nearly as quickly as you can in 1970 or 1980.

MR. DUKAKIS: What do you think the political implications of that fact—this motion of speed now because of television. What does that do to the whole picture?

MR. DEARDOURFF: It creates an incredible amount of uncertainty as to the result. I'm not sure whether it's the cause, but one of my concerns about television is the preoccupation with these wide swings and the fact that we become so wrapped up in who is up and who is down and by how much and the amounts of money that are being spent both privately and publicly to measure these changes. When you start talking about them everybody agrees are not terribly relevant. It begins to infect the whole public attitude about the strengths of these candidates. And it diverts attention in my judgment from the question we began to talk about, and that is how can candidates talk about the issues or whatever else they want to talk about directly with the voters.

How Media Affect Campaigning

MR. DUKAKIS: How does it affect the way candidates talk about issues? What do you advise your clients in the face of this enormous increase in the speed of commercials?

MR. DEARDOURFF: We advise them, if they want to be sure of what reaches voters, that they buy it. They pay for time to say what they want to say. We badger networks and local stations to give us bigger blocks of time. We argue about whether we can have two minutes or three minutes rather than 30 seconds. We attempt to create forums like the debates where you can get an unfiltered communication between the candidates.

MR. DUKAKIS: Does it affect the way your candidate campaigns?

MR. DEARDOURFF: Sure.

MR. DUKAKIS: How?

MR. DEARDOURFF: Every candidate and every staff is acutely aware of all the deadlines of all the media. You're running around constantly making sure you do something for the first editions of the major papers and you've got something to say that makes the wires and making sure you've got another story that's timely enough to be able to be transmitted back to New York to make the evening news. Scheduling, travel, release of information, all of that is designed essentially to accommodate the timetables of the media.

MR. CLYMER: How about substance?

MR. DEARDOURFF: The problem with substance is simply that what is substantive to the New York Times is a bigger dose than other people can absorb. The good campaign is a campaign that tries simultaneously to appeal to the most interested and the best-educated voters and to the least motivated and least well-educated. That means you don't have one campaign, you have a series. In the best campaign, you have a series of campaigns going forward simultaneously, and that is not necessarily ever satisfactory to anybody. It's certainly not satisfactory to the candidates, most of whom, I think, are intelligent, committed people who would like to talk more about issues. They don't have many forums in which to do that, and they also are aware of the overload, the problem of how much in any given day is going to be said about what they say anyway.

It's fascinating to me that the best known media event in Iowa was the commercial that the Baker campaign did. That commercial got 50 times more coverage than the appearance that Baker made at the place where the television commercial was filmed. Now, that's a news judgment. Somebody decided that what he said wasn't important enough to cover. I thought it was important. It was a specific idea that he was proposing which had some meat. It wasn't a major proposal, but it never got really covered in any way until we put it on television.

MR. DUKAKIS: And ran it over and over again. John Marttila, let me ask you a question. The television blunder, Muskie in New Hampshire—did he or didn't he weep? The Roger Mudd interview with Ted Kennedy, George Romney saying, I was brainwashed. Is the television blunder a new factor in presidential politics?

MR. MARTTILA: Sure it is. Television campaigns deal with television as a potential ally and a potential threat. Furthermore, I think the media are somewhat sanctimonious about the attempts of campaigns to present issues to the voters. Campaigns are not totally virtuous works. On the other hand, I have been associated with many candidates who made a serious effort to present substantive policy statements on a variety of issues, and I have seen 100-page research documents presented for solutions on the Middle East and energy crisis and so forth. And there was also a deliberate attempt not to hype it, to present it as a serious substantive statement. It got virtually no coverage. What happens after a while if you have been through this on a regular basis, you begin to deal with television in that you need a good visual. You have to prepare a visual backup to get the story on the evening news, and it does become a bit cynical.

I'm not defending all of the practices that take place inside campaigns; on the other hand I think the true solution to this problem will only come about if the media themselves recognize that their attitudes are a little sanctimonious. I think among the working press there's a lot of cynicism about a piece of research that required enormous effort on the part of the candidate, staff, his research people, and just does not get coverage. Unless you're willing to give some kind of political drama to the event or to get visual backup, you're likely to be blanked out. For television it's a mistake—unless you're talking about a cataclysmic event—not to guarantee some kind of visual background so you conform with local news coverage.

MR. DUKAKIS: Isn't that inherent, however, in the medium, Bill Small? How do you deal with a hundred-page position paper on the Middle East?

Taking a Stand on the Issues

MR. SMALL: I'm amused at John Deardourff's reference to the reliability factor in commercials. He, of course, means reliable to him. John's comment about who is sanctimonious and who is not—every candidate for public office when he goes out to campaign is not interested in issues as such. What he's interested in is getting elected, and he uses issues that way.

If an issue in any given state is going to hurt him, he avoids it. If the President has a State of the Union address that is very hawkish, and there's a patriotic fervor that the politician senses in the land, then he departs from his previous position. Just look at all—with one or two exceptions—of the candidates who normally would be considered liberal doves on an issue such as detente, and see what they have been saying since the State of the Union. And you know the ones I'm talking about.

MR. QUINN: Who? Maybe you should tell us. I'm not sure of this—you covered Jerry Brown since that time he appeared here, the same day as the State of the Union. It was a secret appearance. The hall was far more crowded than today, and if there was a camera here I think it may have been one from the public TV station in Boston. You didn't cover that and you don't really know.

MR. SMALL: I know what he has said and I know what Ted Kennedy has said, and if anything, these are two exceptions. I was thinking primarily of senators like Jacob Javits and Frank Church and others who may indeed resume their political posture, their normal ideological stance, but it's not true this week.

The point I'm making is that politicians with these advisers or any others, or on their own, are not going to take chances unless they perceive some political gain it in. Now, Jerry Brown, John Anderson on the Republican side, and a lot of others have seen that playing the other side might get them attention, and on a lot of issues they go that route. That doesn't mean it isn't useful for the political dialogue. All I'm saying is where they start, and the only thing that matters most to them is getting elected.

MR. CLYMER: That is unduly cynical. There are some candidates who say what they think even when it is explained to them by their pollster that it is a bad idea to say that. Indeed, there was a very considerable argument—I don't know how much Kennedy himself was involved in it—among people who said that when you make the speech, you ought to be to the right of

Carter on foreign policy and to the left of him on domestic policy; and some of the earlier drafts and the memos said the trouble with the Carter policy is we can't get our troops into the Middle East in less than 30 days, we have to have a force to get them there in 10 days.

Now, it's possible to argue that he made his decisions about what ultimately to say just from an analysis of where his base of support had to be. That's one version of it. It's also possible that he said no, I don't want to say that, it might win me some points, but I don't believe it.

I believe candidates do indulge in that sort of thing frequently to the utter distress of some of the people who work for them and are trying to say, look, for the greater good of getting you elected, don't talk about this.

MR. SMALL: I don't deny that in terms of the negative, candidates avoid a subject. But it's pretty rare in the history of American politics where the advisers, or the candidate himself, say take a strong stand on this and you'll get defeated. Take Baker. He says quite candidly on gun control, if you come from Tennessee and are for gun control, you're not going to get reelected to the Senate. He's quite candid about that. But he's not going to come into a state such as this one, where there might be a different reaction, and intentionally endanger his chances by going into that area. He's going to say the things, quite properly from his point of view, that he thinks will get him elected.

MR. DEARDOURFF: I want to make one point about television. I wish that there were some ways—without in any sense implying any criticism, because I don't have any, of the way in which political reporters cover politics, but Adam Clymer has been discussing something here which is kind of an insider's frame of mind about how Ted Kennedy arrived at the decision to say what he was going to say. I wish that we could simply get out as far as we can spread it what he actually said and somehow cut through the very legitimate stories that are written about why he chose to say these words at this place on this particular day and what the arguments were among his staff people about whether he was going to say and how he was going to say it. What tends to get lost is what he said. That's what I'm arguing for. I wish we could work out some way that would permit a candidate a certain amount of time to speak directly to people rather than through this filter which always is interested in the question not of what he says, but why did he pick Waterloo, Iowa, on Tuesday, January 3, to talk about this subject. You'll find, if you go back and look at political reports of these speeches—print and television—you're going to get a lot of what I call double-think about why these things happened rather than what happened.

MR. DUKAKIS: Bill Small, why do you always pay attention to the unimportant things?

MR. DEARDOURFF: I don't want to suggest that at all. I'm simply saying let's add to that the possibility of somehow allowing viewers to know precisely what the candidate wants to say.

MR. SMALL: Let me say a word in defense of filters. Is it not true that the Kennedy Georgetown speech was carried on prime time in the Northeast?

MR. LYDON: Yes.

MR. SMALL: His entire speech was seen in his next targets, if you will, in Massachusetts and New Hampshire. On the question of our filtering, I think it is as important to our viewers that professional journalists have an opportunity to observe what you're doing as it is for them to hear what you want them to hear.

MR. DEARDOURFF: I couldn't agree more.

MR. SMALL: Even on the question of commercials, it's an interesting thing that has happened in television news, that really just since 1976—although there were some attempts in 1964 on the daisy commercial—one of the things that we do with increasing frequency is to analyze the image-making and the commercials, including Baker's Iowa commercial. So commercials are now expected as part of news stories, which takes it still another dimension.

MR. QUINN: Next time somebody will produce a commercial just for that reason. I think I made my point. I think there's a dangerous process going on here that none of us is very sensitive to. I think the media is having a very difficult time, particularly television, covering politics because of the time limitations primarily, not because of bad faith or lack of effort. Thirty minutes, even though that may be more time than most people would want to watch, isn't enough time to do the kind of coverage that probably Bill Small would like to do. But I expect in fact he would have a better program, more satisfying program for himself, for his staff, for his journalists, I think for the public, if he had an hour, for example.

But, that's one problem. The other problem is there's a manipulation of the press, particularly television, that goes on by candidates. The kind of series drama that Chris Lydon discussed is possible, easier for incumbents than nonincumbents, but possible. We went through that in California to some extent in 1978, Gov. Brown's reelection. The day after the primary election he was one point ahead in polls. He ended up winning a couple of months later by the largest margin in the history of the state. Why? Because there was a psychodrama, Proposition 13—it doesn't compare to Iran and Afghanistan—but in California it was a major story. Every night there were events taking place in Sacramento. It was in one sense scripted out prior to the election when it became obvious that Prop. 13 was going to pass. Preparations were made for legislation to implement Prop. 13, but there was an effort also to sell our legislative package to the legislature and the public, there was a planned press conference on this date, a proclamation written, executive orders drafted, a TV address planned for a certain date, an address to the joint session of the legislature, all before Prop. 13 passed.

MR. SMALL: And a 180-degree turn on his position.

MR. QUINN: What I'm saying is that to some extent we took advantage of incumbency to get the excessive—

MR. DUKAKIS: You took advantage of incumbency, sure you did, and you scripted it out, worked hard and won by a big margin. Proposition 13 was your Iran, wasn't it?

MR. QUINN: No one was killed there.

MR. DUKAKIS: To be sure, but in the same terms. You did it. I don't think anyone looks askance at that.

MR. QUINN: It's a mistake. But the fact is Iran rehabilitated Jimmy Carter. Whether or not he created it, certainly he's doing a masterful job at least on television of handling the situation. And I'm just suggesting that that's something that all of us have to worry about.

A Legal Problem

MR. DUKAKIS: That's an important question. How do you deal with it?

MR. SMALL: Let me make a point on the first thing that Tom said, which is terribly important, that is the amount of time available. Because one of the things we've overlooked is what we ourselves as a nation have done to television by imposing the equal time provision. Section 315 limits what we can do to regularly scheduled newscasts, regularly scheduled interviews and bona fide news events. So when you get into a campaign, at all the networks there is a great appetite to do more broadcast relating to campaign, but you're prohibited because of equal time.

MR. CLYMER: You could have covered the Iowa debate.

MR. SMALL: The Iowa debate, of course, could have been covered and originally the plan was to cover it because the inspiration for covering it wasn't every Republican except Reagan. The inspiration was that an incumbent President for the first time was going to debate prior to a primary. No precedent. It was an event of major news importance. The kind of forum that resulted, while I agree with you, it was important and well run, wasn't quite the same animal and we will see a series of these forums. Some of them will be covered locally, some of them will be covered by public broadcasting, some may indeed be covered by the networks.

But what we cannot do is devote special programming to political campaigns. In 1968 CBS wanted to do an hour on George Wallace because it looked like he was emerging as a spoiler who might throw the election into the House of Representatives. The only way you could do that is by never showing George Wallace except incidentally. Now, I don't know how you do an hour on a candidate and never hear from him or show him. But 315 prevented it.

We did an NBC White Paper in December on the American presidency. By law we could only make incidental use of an incumbent President because he's up for reelection. So our lawyers determined that incidental use meant three minutes or whatever it was over a 90-minute broadcast. You could not interview the incumbent President in depth because you were in a campaign.

Right now the Congress is toying with the idea of amending 315. It ought to be abolished. It is in my mind a clear violation of the First Amendment. But we have been living under it all these years.

MR. DUKAKIS: Should we abolish the equal time rule?

MR. DEARDOURFF: I think so.

MR. DUKAKIS: Does that trouble anybody around the table?

MR. QUINN: It troubles me. I think these are public air waves. Stations are licensed to operate in the public interest, convenience, and necessity. There is potential for abuse. I'm not saying we see it, but there's potential for abuse by a broadcaster who may in fact favor candidates for partisan reasons or their own personal reasons. I think 315 provides a useful check. I do think the networks have a lot of flexibility within 315. They could have, if they wish, an hour network newscast every night at 11:30 if they wish, all exempted from 315.

MR. SMALL: If you start an 11:30 newscast now already in the presidential campaign, there is a very serious legal question of the exemption . . . .

MR. QUINN: You clearly could expand the NBC Nightly News to an hour without any 315 problem.

MR. CLYMER: I think the answer to the 315 question is quite simple. Yes, for all the unkind things I have said about television news coverage, I would trust the three major television networks without 315. But I am far from convinced that I would trust every little television station here, there, and in the country not to promote a candidate.

MR. SMALL: The First Amendment doesn't say that there will be a free press except for those small station owners who dislike a candidate or dislike an issue.

MR. CLYMER: You haven't won your case that the First Amendment protects you. Maybe you should, but you have lost that case in the courts.

MR. SMALL: That's right and the courts are wrong and ultimately I think we will see that prevail. If not, this country is in very serious shape, because if you look at the pattern of where people get their news and you see the curve continuing upward in television, that's pretty frightening if there isn't the full protection of the First Amendment.

And when you say there may be abuses on the local level, I have no doubt there are, just as there are abuses in local newspapers, including very large newspapers in this country. But the First Amendment recognizes that this will exist. That's not a problem.

MR. LYDON: Go back to the point Bill Small made. You talk about television news now making news pieces out of how the commercial manipulating the process might be done. But in public television we sit back on a night like the Iowa caucuses and we will do analyses of how commercial news manipulates the media. We discuss how to make an interesting political commercial for somebody like Howard Baker, who didn't win in Iowa. We are free to analyze and do a piece on what happened when NBC moves Chancellor out to Des Moines and Cronkite goes out and I don't know how many million of bucks you put into the apparatus, electronic stuff, Tom Brokaw, Frank Reynolds, the whole bit. That is infinitely more important, infinitely more powerful manipulation of the political process. It's not evil, but simply the weight that Cronkite had to come up with, the finality, the heaviness of the news, the celebration of George Bush who barely beat Ronald Reagan, but you find out he had reinvented the wheel in Iowa. A star was born in the cornfields.

MR. SMALL: Your basic point is correct that part of the story is indeed the influence of the media on caucuses. On the Today show, the morning after, if I recall correctly, Jim Gannon of the Des Moines Register, dealing with this very subject, said the heavy turnout in Iowa and the good behavior on the part of our voters was because all you heavyweights were coming in and looking at it. Listen, that's been New Hampshire's gig for as long as I have been alive. They had the first primary and they love the attention.

MR. LYDON: But it's different, really is different in the sense that in the old days—I mean even 20 years ago—the candidate had to go and deal with leaders. He doesn't have to do that now. In the John Kennedy era there was good deal more of dealing with leadership and groups. That faded under television.

In the 1960s antiwar period one had to have an organizing issue. In the latest period we would really be better off if we simply realize what you've got to do now is be a TV character.

Summing Up

MR. DUKAKIS: I'm not sure I can sum up very effectively except to say there's general consensus around the table that television has made a major difference. It costs a lot more money, it raises all kinds of very difficult problems for people who have to make those decisions, who are responsible for television news, and it's clearly had an effect on candidate behavior.

ROUNDTABLE FOUR

Covering the Issues

MODERATOR

Newton N. Minow, chairman of the Federal Communications Commission from 1961 to 1963, is now with the Chicago law firm of Sidley and Austin and serves on the boards of directors of five corporations. He is also chairman of the Public Broadcasting Service and holds several other civic and public service directorships. Mr. Minow received a doctorate in law from Northwestern University and was clerk to U.S. Chief Justice Fred M. Vinson. He was administrative assistant to Illinois Gov. Adlai E. Stevenson in 1952 and 1953.

PANELISTS

Alan Baron is publisher of the Baron Report, a Washington-based political newsletter. He also is a former aide to Sen. George S. McGovern (D-S.D.) and worked with the 1972 presidential campaign of Sen. Edmund S. Muskie (D-Maine).

James Doyle is deputy chief of Newsweek magazine's Washington bureau.

Peter D. Hart is president of Peter D. Hart Research Associates Inc., which has been polling for Sen. Edward M. Kennedy (D-Mass.). Mr. Hart has worked for numerous Democratic campaigns, including that of Rep. Morris K. Udall (D-Ariz.) in 1976.

Haynes Johnson is a columnist for the Washington Post.

Jess Marlow is a correspondent and anchorman for KNBC-TV News in Los Angeles.

David A. Stockman is a U.S. congressman from Michigan's 4th District. He formerly was an aide to U.S. Rep. John B. Anderson (D-Ill.).

ROUNDTABLE FOUR

A Perspective on 1980; Assessing Media Performance; Cynicism in the Press Corps; How Issues Affect Politics; The Limits of Television; Problems With the Press; The Carter-Bush Phonomenon; Real and Imagined Liabilities; Polls and the Shaping of Opinion; The Dynamics of the Process; Understanding the Issues; Summing Up.

A Perspective on 1980

NEWTON N. MINOW: When we think about covering the issues, I am reminded of a famous story that happened at my city of Chicago. Mayor Daley was walking along the lake one day with Cardinal Cody, head of the Catholic Church in our archdiocese. The Cardinal was wearing his red hat, and it was a windy day and his hat blew off into the lake. He was alarmed about it, but Mayor Daley said, Don't worry about it, Cardinal, I'll get it for you." He walked out across the water, fetched the hat, and brought it back. A Sun-Times reporter happened to see the incident, and the next day the Sum-Times said in a big headline, "Daley can't swim." (Laughter)

That's the way we cover the issues sometimes in politics. I thought we might begin with some questions from the Los Angeles Times Poll. I'm going to read you three questions and the answers and then I'm going to read you a fourth question.

How much do you think you learned about the various candidates during their campaigns for the nomination? Do you think you learned a lot or a little about whether you can trust them? Sixteen percent say a lot, 77 percent say a little.

Next question, do you think you learned a lot or a little about whether they are able to run the country effectively? Fourteen percent say a lot, 76 percent say a little.

Do you think you learned a lot or a little about how they will solve the important problems of the country? Sixteen percent say a lot, 73 percent say a little.

Then another question is, taking everything in consideration, would you say that press coverage of the way candidates are chosen is very good, fairly good, fairly bad, or very bad? The answer, 85 percent good, 11 percent bad.

It seems to me what the public is saying in the poll is that, even though we are not learning too much, we are pretty well satisfied. Peter Hart, do you think that's right or is that the way you read the opinion these days?

PETER D. HART: I guess if I were talking about where the country is and looking at things and trying to put into perspective what the issues are really all about in terms of 1980, you can talk about the three major issues, the first being inflation/the economy, the second being energy, and the third being foreign policy.

But after the 1980 election is really all over, it's going to be Teddy White's job to sum up what 1980 was all about, and I don't think you have to wait until it's all over. The problem is that we sort of misunderstand how the issues are used and how they relate to a campaign. And what I say the 1980 campaign is really all about is order and stability. People see their lives as out of control, and the issues that are confronting us as somewhat out of control. Whether it be energy, inflation or foreign policy, it's a matter of controlling; they want a certain amount of reassurance as to what's going on. So consequently that's where all the candidates will be headed. And the way in which they use the issues is not going to be on individual items, but instead it's going to be a vehicle to tell you what the candidate's all about. I know that the League of Women Voters would like to have you believe that the voter is out there deciding on the individual issues and making some very definite decisions. But people don't really decide on individual issues, they decide much more in terms of general character and how people are going to use the presidency and what the presidency is all about.

Take a look at 1968. Eugene McCarthy ran in New Hampshire as a one-issue candidate, a peace candidate, and that was the single most dominant issue. Yet it was determined right after the New Hampshire primary that over half the people who voted for Eugene McCarthy did not know his stand on the Vietnam War or thought he was a hawk, either one.

And I would say that issues sort of delineate people maybe as extremist or nonextremist, as the case may be. I would say that Goldwater, McGovern and Wallace probably all got cast as "extremist" and most of the other candidates were not cast as extremist.

So as I see the issues role, it's delineating the character, it tells us what they are all about. But the issues go a little beyond that. The issues have the ability to raise money for a candidate with a specific stand. It energizes and mobilizes volunteers, who are terribly important. And the third thing I would say is that it provides some sort of rationale for the press to tell you how you're different.

So that's how I see the framework of the issues. I don't see them as individual items like a smorgasbord that people are picking up, but I'm saying they get one overall impression of a person by the issues he chooses and the way in which he approaches them.

Assessing Media Performance

MR. MINOW: I'm going to ask the congressman, who serves on the subcommittee in the House that is dealing with energy and working night and day to agree on a national energy policy, knowing as much as you do about the issue, do you feel that the campaign and the way the media reports the issue is adequate? Do you feel it's accurate?

REP. DAVID A. STOCKMAN: You have to start by asking, compared to what? When you discuss this whole thing you have a serious problem of definition. In my view, issues are relatively simple. Policy analysis is fairly complex. And legislative drafting and regulation writing is a form of Chinese water torture of the mind. And the question is, do campaigns function as a policy seminar at Harvard or as a drafting session to put legislation together? And my answer is no, and that the way issues are used in a campaign is to convey a basic sense of the candidate's posture or attitude about government and about major constellations of issues, whether it's the economy or energy and so forth.

In that context, I think energy is being covered fairly well in this campaign, and I don't really have any sort of stirring critique about why you don't get into details of how you strike the windfall profits tax and what kind of price controls Kennedy wants to reimpose on oil. I don't think that's a relevant part of campaign communication process.

It's important enough for the voters to know that Kennedy wants to put on controls, because that says he thinks the oil companies are causing the problem and that that's where the solution lies. It's equally important for Connally or Bush or one of the others to say they are totally opposed to controls and want to dismantle DOE because the problem is largely a result of bureaucratic interference, controls and so forth.

Some people feel that's too superficial, but it conveys important messages that register with people in terms of their basic disposition. So in that sense I think it's relevant.

MR. MINOW: Jim Doyle, you have the luxury of not having a daily deadline. Phil Graham once said that the news magazines were a first draft of history. Do you think Newsweek is doing a good job on the issues?

JAMES DOYLE: It's an unfair question. The answer inside the magazine is no, and I guess I have to admit that. I agree with what David Stockman said, but I don't think that the medium integrates discussion of the issues with discussion of the campaign well enough. As a matter of fact and as a matter of advantage we probably do it better than television. I think we even do it better than the daily newspapers in terms of campaign stories. But what bothers me is that Newsweek magazine has made it clear over the past two years that the overriding issues that they think face this country and its leadership are the three things that Peter Hart mentioned: the economic problems in the world specifically as they impact on this country; the energy problems of the world and, again, specifically as they impact on government policy in this country and on the economy of this country, and thirdly, our foreign policy or lack of, where we are headed, why, and whether there's any rationality behind where we are coming from as we come out of the Vietnam period.

We have done a number of covers on all these issues. In fact on the energy issue, Newsweek magazine last summer did what we call an advocacy cover for the second time in its history. Only on the civil rights issue of the 1960s and energy, has Newsweek done a cover called "What Must Be Done." We separated out the journalism role and we advocated solutions.

In the campaign coverage we did a Bush cover this week. There is not a section in there saying Bush does or doesn't agree with us on the things we said about what must be done about energy.

It's early, but I think there are structural problems with coverage of campaigns that make it very difficult to integrate discussion of the issues so that when you get the opportunity to discuss energy—when George Bush on an airplane between here and Iowa passes out a 15-page energy statement because he's going into a forum there where this will be useful—the reporter is able to sit down, read it, collate it and compare it with others and do a discursive piece which says: Bush on energy, this is where it stands, this is how it compares to other people.

What I would like to see happen is that the airplanes get abolished so that reporters are not stuck in that capsule where they cannot report in a definitive way on the issues and are not tempted to try to do it so that we end up getting stories. What typically happens is you get a story saying Ronald Reagan yesterday shot himself in the foot when he said the following. Which is important, what he said or that it's a tactical mistake? That happens all the time. We did a lot of that in 1976. What did the ethnic purity debate tell us about the Carter presidency? What did the "lust in my heart" remark, which Bob Scheer inveigled out of him in a long interview, tell us about the Carter presidency or whether Jimmy Carter was a hypocrite or not? I would maintain zero. But they became sort of running stories, gauntlet stories for a week or 10 days, the second one at a critical time in the campaign when people were trying to decide on Carter's character. It was an important story and I don't think there was enough reflection about whether we should have done that.

Cynicism in the Press Corps

MR. MINOW: The question you raise I want to really put in a way to Haynes Johnson. One thing I have picked up about the first three panels from people who are not journalists is astonishment and horror at the level of cynicism on the part of the press.

It was even suggested, for example, that the President may have deliberately sought to have the hostages taken in Iran to advance his political career. That level of cynicism has, as I say, shocked us. We, the consumers of the information about the issues, have to get our information through your filters. Is there, because of Watergate and Vietnam, a high level of cynicism in the press corps?

HAYNES JOHNSON: I don't know. You're from Chicago. I guess we are all spiritual descendants of the press of Hildy Johnson, who was much more cynical than many of my contemporaries. That was the old "Front Page" character with an egg-stained shirt and bottle of whiskey on the desk who was cynical about everybody. I don't think that's necessarily true. I think it's nonsense the idea that Carter manufactured the hostages.

We, the press, are always looking for *the* issue. We are always trying to find *the* issue. If you go back to 1960, the missile gap was the issue. That was a fake. Then in 1964 it was who had the finger on the button. Then in 1968 we had the wonderful secret plan to win the war, Nixon's way to get us out of the war. It was a secret plan. In 1972, when we all were writing learned stories about the great issues of that campaign being ideological—we had the three A's, acid, abortion, amnesty. And then in 1976 I guess we had the spirit of America. I'm not sure what that played out to be. Now it seems to be the flag. If you don't wave it, you're a defiler of the flag. That seems to be where 1980 is so far. I think what Peter Hart is saying is right: people are judging not on one thing but on what they perceive to be the person's ability to handle these terrible problems they know exist.

I remember in 1972 when George Wallace was doing so well in the primaries. He was winning one primary after another; if you remember, he had won two the day before he was shot. One of the fascinating things to me about talking to voters then was the voters who were voting for Wallace in the primaries would tell you they would never vote for him for president. They were making a very distinct judgment. They didn't like the way things were going in Washington, they wanted to register a protest, not only about the direction of the country, but they also were choosing a president that day. They didn't want George Wallace in there; they thought he was unstable, he was dangerous. They were somehow looking at the character of the man who would be in that job. It's a much more complicated process than we convey, and I don't know what the answers are, but I don't think we are doing a very good job about reporting the issues nor even delineating the character, which is a much more difficult one.

MR. MINOW: Alan Baron, your clientele are the people running all these campaigns. How much do they care about the issues?

How Issues Affect Politics

ALAN BARON: I think the ones who do care about the issues in the broad est sense of the word and have an understanding of how issues affect politics are the ones very likely to be successful in them. The voters are a pretty sophisticated group of people who know what they are doing when they go in and vote.

In some elections, not this year, but Democratic and Republican races so far, they go in, as Haynes Johnson said, to send a message, whether it's for Gene McCarthy or George Wallace. The voters were using their votes to go in and send a message to the country and to the media and to the governing officials. In 1972 in the Democratic primary in Florida, George Wallace came in first with 42 percent of the vote and the candidate I was working for, Ed Muskie, came in fourth with nine percent of the vote. And as the voters walked out of the polling booth these Democrats were asked who they would support in the general election between Wallace and Nixon and Jackson and Nixon and Muskie and Nixon and McGovern and Nixon. And only one candidate was able to come anywhere near Richard Nixon among Democrats. In fact only one was able to beat Nixon among Democrats. That was Muskie, who came in fourth.

But they weren't electing a president that day. They were sending a message, and they sent a message for Wallace as they did for McCarthy. This year the people in Iowa—and the media had something to do with this, it wasn't a technical thing so much—decided this was serious business, they were choosing a president. And in choosing a president, issues are important to the extent that people perceive or try to perceive how the candidates relate to them and to what they want in a president.

It's been said time and time again here that George Bush won Iowa because he spent 28 days in Iowa and got a lot of organizers and did a great job. Well, I don't know the numbers, but Phil Crane I'm sure did about as much work as George Bush did in Iowa. In 1976 Fred Harris and Mo Udall and Birch Bayh did a lot of work in Iowa. You don't win voters by shaking their hands only. It's important, but I think Phil Crane could walk into the room here and spend 10 hours shaking hands, talking to people, conversing with them, and probably not carry this audience here.

The fact is you've got to start with the product. In 1976 Jimmy Carter, better than any other candidate running, understood where the country was, what people wanted in the president. Time and time again I heard in 1976 from people who were supporting Jimmy Carter in Iowa—more than this popular stuff, we want a manager, we don't want a congressman or senator, we want a governor who knows how to get things done.

You heard that again and again, and Jimmy Carter gave it back to them.

This year, had George Bush gotten 25 percent in Iowa and Reagan 30, I still would have argued that Reagan was down. George Bush reflected—I'm from Iowa—the Republicans in Iowa that I grew up with. They are a little bit more moderate and not as strident as Reagan on social issues. They are fiscal conservatives. The qualities they look for in a candidate most are stability and maturity. They are conservatives with a small c but they're not reactionaries. They don't want to change things too fast. They want that kind of guy to run their business. George Bush fit that. If he hadn't fit that, he wouldn't have run in Iowa as well as he did. I talked with Bush's media guy yesterday, Bobby Goodman. He said Bush and Carter had a tremendous opportunity. Since neither one of them holds public office they could read the polls, they could find out what the people wanted, they were totally unknown when they began their campaigns. And to some extent, as very bright, intelligent men, they were able to shape the images that they conveyed according to what the public wanted.

They started like you're designing a product. They didn't start with Tide, they started with brand X and designed it according to what those people wanted. In that kind of situation, can somebody who goes into the race very identifiable—I mean somebody like Henry Jackson or Morris Udall or Ronald Reagan or John Connally or Edward Kennedy, with strong liabilities and deficits in a public record—can they mold themselves or do they just have to wait until they happen to get lucky enough to find a year in which the public wants their kind of candidate? If they don't wait, which is where the odds are, they don't make it.

That's the issue: Are we going to find a new guy each year who is able to create an image? Doesn't that create a tremendous obligation for the press, which maybe we don't fulfill, to go back and really look into Bush's record, into Carter's record, into each person's record and everything they have done in public life. That wasn't done with Carter. When it *was* done in 1976 it was ignored and called unfair.

If Edward Kennedy had distributed brochures in Massachusetts in the busing area which were clearly racist in nature, it would have been on the front page of every paper. Jimmy Carter did it in Georgia with brochures of Carl Sanders dancing with a black woman at the inaugural ball. But those were ignored because that happened in Georgia, and it doesn't really make any difference. How tough do we get, to go back to these guys' records when they are unknown?

The Limits of Television

MR. DOYLE: They weren't ignored. The fact is that the medium becomes important, and that's why there was so much discussion of television. They were ignored by television because it's very difficult on television to use that.

In 1976 right after the nomination Newsweek did that cover, which we called the "big Jimmy cover." We had sent about 10 people down into Georgia and had gone over all of that stuff. I don't think we do enough of it. It gets to the question of character very much, and it gets to the question of whether the issues get delineated. I think David Stockman is absolutely right that you can do shorthand on issues. But are you going to talk about Jimmy Carter and how he ran that campaign in 1970 or whenever it was, or are you going to talk about the things that are important to the country, and how do you play these things off?

If Phil Jones had been covering Jimmy Carter and during a major speech had said, of course this is the same Jimmy Carter whose campaign distributed literature of Carl Sanders dancing with a black woman, everyone would have said that's an outrageous piece of television; it's like the TelePrompTer remark he made on the Kennedy thing. You can't do it that way. You have structural problems.

MR. MINOW: Speaking of television, Jess Marlow reaches millions of people every night. When you go home at the end of the day and you're thinking about your conscience, do you think there's something you should have done differently or not? Are you satisfied with the way you're handling the issues?

JESS MARLOW: Of course not, especially when it comes to handling the issues. As Alan Baron points out, the media generally deal with images more than issues, and television specifically deals more with images than issues. We leave images, we leave impressions. I don't think we deal sufficiently with the issues. It does concern me if we are doing two hours and our competitor is doing two and a half. You would think that in that amount of time we would have ample opportunity to deal with all these issues well.

Part of it is not just limitation of time. I might add that our two-hour newscast is almost two one-hour newscasts back to back. We don't assume we have the entire audience for that whole two hours. It's a bit like all-news radio where people do tune in and out. And we want while they are there for them to get the major stories of the day. So there is some redundancy built into that.

But even given this luxury of time which we in Los Angeles have, we do not deal sufficiently with lots of the issues because of some inherent weakness in the medium. We cover politicians very well, but I don't think we cover politics very well.

We can cover a presidential campaign fairly well, but we do not cover the issues of energy, the issues of inflation, the economy. We don't cover those stories well at all, partly because they are statistical stories that ought to be read and digested carefully, maybe even ought to be studied. And television is not studied, it's watched.

That's one of the great differences. Having said that and having acknowledged our great weakness, even as I look at the statistics in the Los Angeles Times Poll, I still insist the audience voting today is better informed than the audience that voted a generation ago, even given this glaring weakness, because at least they have some awareness of images, of impressions, some awareness of issues. Past generations voted on the basis of party line, and now at least voters know who the candidate is and at least part of what he stands for.

The electorate is better informed than ever before but still woefully inadequately informed.

MR. MINOW: We have had two national presidential debates. The man that organized the one in 1960, Frank Stanton, happens to be here today. In 1976 I was the cochairman for the League of Women Voters for the debates. After the debates I'd be interviewed on television, and people would ask, why was it so boring, why was it so dull; who won, who lost? I'd say, you're missing the point. You had the two candidates speaking for 90 minutes on issues so the public could make a choice on the issues. But they said it was boring. What's your answer to that?

Do you have to have people constantly fighting with each other to make an interesting television political program?

MR. MARLOW: We in television suffer from several cliches; one of them is "vast wasteland." Another is "talking head." It is one of our big problems that we have conditioned ourselves to believe that a talking head is uninteresting. The truth is there are some damned interesting talking heads. Some of them are right here. But we still insist everything has to be visually exciting. The only way we made the energy issue of visual interest was when we looked at Three Mile Island. I hope we don't have to have that in politics, to develop some interesting issues. But it is not visually an interesting picture. While we've been conditioned to believe talking heads are dull, I'm afraid we have also conditioned our audience to think that, and perhaps we ought to reconsider too.

The presidential debates were really not dull, if you cared at all about the process, at all about the system, at all about the candidates. They should not have been dull. Maybe that audience that only learns 16 percent gets precisely what it wants.

MR. MINOW: The Iowa debate was not carried by commercial television live, it was carried by public broadcasting. I happened to be with Congressman John Anderson not long ago and he told me if it hadn't been for the fact that it was carried on public broadcasting nobody would know who he was. We have got to find a way for candidates to have some additional access to television. We talked a little of that in the other panels. What is your feeling about the way a candidate currently has to buy time? Should there be some requirement, where he has access to time, that he explain his views on the issues in more than 30 seconds?

MR. MARLOW: I would love for him to have the opportunity. I'm not sure that you ought to require it, but they should provide opportunities in longer newscasts. There's really no justification for the network newscast being 30 minutes. It really should be expanded, certainly into the hour that any decent local station now does. In our local newscast we provide a five-minute live interview each day generally during the political season. Certainly that could be done and ought to be encouraged.

MR. HART: If you go back to the Iowa debate, I really felt the Republican Party was the big winner out of that debate because they did not look like Neanderthals and by and large you could say that's a fairly attractive panel of people. They may or may not win your vote, but you didn't feel you were looking at people that were from the 18th Century, and some of the perceptions of the Republican Party are that way.

Correspondingly, the Democratic Party would obviously benefit. We always think about debates in strategic terms: You don't debate when you're ahead, you debate when you're behind . . . But the fact of the matter is, it is one of the best methods of confrontational politics. And that's really what we get down to. There are so few ways that we can understand a person in a confrontational situation. That's what press conferences are all about. You say this person performs well under confrontation and that's when it's not rehearsed and when you get to see a person reacting to a question which obviously has not been given to him directly. You get to see some side of his character.

I remember Mary McGrory's question where she said, is there anything in your past that you really wish that you had done differently? And Phil Crane started apologizing for his dog and for his treatment to his wife and children. It was an interesting answer, but the fact is it gives you a chance of looking at it, let's say, unvarnished, fresh, and getting some sense of what this person is all about.

Again, you come out of any single encounter with one impression. You really don't come out of it with he stood here and here and here and here and here on issues. You put it all back together and you say I like him, I don't like him, this is what he's about.

Problems With The Press

MR. JOHNSON: The question of access isn't just television, it's also just as much in the written press. Every four years there's a battle to get the name in there. I think what my colleague Dave Broder writes has enormous influence on what television does. If Dave decides that someone is really worth watching and devotes some time and space to it, that's very important. There's always the battle to get yourself out there known. There's a game that's being played. I don't think it helps the process very much, but we are all captives of the game. I don't know the way out of it, but it's more and more complicated each time and more and more difficult. I remember when Dave and I did a survey of voters around the country in 1971 and ranked Democratic prospects. I got a telephone call when we got back. George McGovern had called and said, I didn't even see figures for me, where did I rate? I had to say we didn't put his name on because we had decided that he was not a credible candidate. He became the nominee of the Democratic Party one year later. Carter could have done the same thing.

MR. HART: That's the whole problem with the press—you're always going to fight the last war. In other words, it's never a question of, okay, where are we in 1980 and what is this election battle really all about. Now, let's figure out how we are going to deploy it. What happened is the New York Times and Johnny Apple were out there in Iowa, and he picked up something before anybody else, and by and large while people weren't picking up Carter, what happened is he was, let's say, on the crest on that one. So what happens in 1980 is everyone troops down to Florida and says we are not going to miss this one, so we are going to fight it by the past. It's the same thing.

MR. DOYLE: I think that's completely wrong on who trooped down to Florida. The candidates trooped down; we followed them down. Someone said to me, how many people does Newsweek have in Florida? I said we had four. They said, if the networks weren't here and the dailies weren't here, how many would you have? I said we'd have about 10 or 12. That was a very good story. It would have been a much better story had we been the only ones onto it. Johnny Apple got a lot of credit for what happened in Iowa in 1976 and maybe he deserves it. I think we learned something from the Florida straw vote. A tremendous number of people—including Dade County, which was supposed to be Kennedy's stronghold—turned out and a lot of them voted against him on a day when it was raining like crazy. That was an important story, and it should have been covered well. The stories all made the point that no delegates were being selected, that the process is starting earlier, and that in fact it may turn out to be debilitating to the delegate selection process. It's going to turn out that it's not that debilitating because Iowa—it's different than other caucuses—became a situation where a large number of people took part in the political process. It will probably strengthen the two parties out there. The Florida thing probably strengthened the parties down there.

MR. BARON: I think Florida was an important event. I went last June to cover a draft Kennedy rally in Minneapolis. There were people that came in from all over the country, and I called Minneapolis liberals who had been for McCarthy and who had been active in the Muskie campaign and other campaigns like that—people who should have been for Kennedy, people who if

Kennedy was going to take off should have been in—but they stayed away.

It was partially that Mondale was from Minnesota, but there were other reasons. That was a sign. Florida was another sign. I think a big problem at least in assessing my own performance in ignoring some of those signs at times was the polls, because you go to a meeting in Minneapolis, you see something in Florida and the polls would still tell us Kennedy was ahead 60 to 30 even though it didn't feel right. Two weeks before he announced I was talking to college students and recent graduates of college, liberals who should have been for Kennedy. You would have expected them to be there and they weren't there.

Florida conveyed something not so much in Carter's vote because he got his vote organizationally, but it conveyed that people, minorities and Jews and senior citizens and other people that the Kennedy camp had expected to rally to them weren't going to do it. Maybe they could get it out by organization, but they weren't rallying.

In 1968, 75,000 people came out in Iowa to vote for Gene McCarthy without one minute of national TV time covering it, with almost no state TV time covering it, with very little publicity, McCarthy spending half a day in the state and $10,000 in total budget. More people came out to vote for McCarthy or as many as voted for Jimmy Carter this year, almost as many as voted in the caucuses.

It wasn't first in the nation. There was a reason they didn't come out for Kennedy this year in Florida, and we should have seen those signs. I think network TV can do more. We had an hour program by Roger Mudd which was with Sen. Kennedy, a very important television program. And I think it had a pretty major impact on the thinking of politicians in America. And on the public.

We haven't had an hour program on Jerry Brown because he's not important enough. We have had a lot of time on Jimmy Carter. We haven't had an hour program like that on Ronald Reagan. I traveled with Ronald Reagan two weeks or three weeks before he announced for the presidency, and I was the only reporter on board the plane.

We haven't had an hour program on George Bush. It seems to me, in giving licenses to TV stations and in making the resources that we make available, we can expect from TV stations hour-long programs on seven or eight major candidates at some point fairly early in September and October. I think the public has a right to expect that, not just on Edward Kennedy but on the others.

MR. DOYLE: That's a more important point than the business about access with the debates. In the case of the Iowa Republican debate, I don't know how good the PBS coverage was. Obviously it was as good as any independent network could have.

As long as there is access in all the major markets, I don't think that the debates have to be carried compulsively by all the stations. That was a terrific debate because it wasn't a debate; it was an open-ended conversation with all these people, and as Peter Hart pointed out, some off-the-wall questions drew some interesting answers.

What's much more important is this sort of thing, the Roger Mudd story. That was an hour that evoked a whole lot of different things and is part of the campaign literature now. Why haven't the networks done that sort of thing? And it's not just the networks, but there are these structural problems of covering the candidates day by day. All the different media have to figure out how to get around those structural problems so that the part of your audience which wants to tune in whichever way you do tune in and pay attention gets the chance to do so. And that's what I think that David Stockman has not completely solved in his discussion about the way you can do things in shorthand. Inflation is a good example. There was a seminar at the Institute of Politics last week about how political reporters cover inflation. The fact is most of them don't know much about economics, etc., but they need to know that so they can ask the right second question. How are you going to do that so the expectations for inflation can be realistic in reporting?

The Carter-Bush Phenomenon

MR. STOCKMAN: Let me expound on that, because I think this opens up a dimension of a problem or a lack of real responsibility on the part of the press to deal with a very specific problem. Apparently because of the nominating process we are getting a new phenomenon, a Carter-Bush phenomenon. It's a very thin public record. You can go out on the campaign trail and use the shorthand messages—which are about the only way to communicate with the public on the issues of a political campaign—and those shorthand messages can be shaped and massaged and structured on the basis of the profile that Alan Baron was talking about.

Now, if you take an incumbent or a senator like Bob Dole, who has been around a long time, or even Reagan, who was a governor and has been stating things on the public record and doing things on the public ledger for a long time, he can't change his spots very easily, he can't change his shorthand. If Teddy Kennedy came out tomorrow and said, I'm going to decontrol everything in the energy field as soon as I'm inaugurated, it wouldn't be credible, the press would jump all over him and he would have a serious problem.

But the Bush and Carter type candidates have to be pursued when they emit these shorthand kinds of messages on inflation or energy or international security policy much more vigorously in order to flesh out what they really mean. Carter said in 1976 he was going to be a manager, going to roll back this overgrown bureaucracy we have, going to cut down the number of government agencies. He should have been pinned down as to what ones he was going to cut out. If any other candidate in 1976 had said that, there was a record to look at. If Jackson had said that, you could see what he had voted for over the years. It seems to me the press is being negligent here, and you have a particular responsibility because of the way issues work and because of the thin candidate who has moved into this nominating process.

MR. DOYLE: You wait and see what will happen to George Bush if he wins a couple of more times. Not that people will pin down where he stands on five or six or three tremendous issues facing the country, but that he will shoot himself in the foot, and that will turn out to be a Playboy interview or something like that, and we will be off and running on that kind of thing. After all, Ted Kennedy got much more publicity for what he said about the Shah. The problem with that was not the first-day stories, but that there were no second-day stories saying there is a policy question here. And everyone left it for the politicians to do and normally they do. In this case they all sat around and told us off the record this is a case when the emperor has no clothes, and when somebody does try criticizing Carter, then the fat is going to be in the fire.

Real and Imagined Liabilities

MR. JOHNSON: Going back to how you judge the character, I was with Reagan this week. I kept hearing him make in a standard speech—it's a red-meat speech and it's designed to draw the audience—a remark about Carter and Communism and softness on Communism. He said that, when Jimmy Carter arrived in Poland at the end of 1977, in Warsaw, he stepped out and the startled satrap of that Communist nation was amazed to hear the President tell him that our concept of human rights is preserved in Poland.

That's a direct quote. I kept hearing this all week and something was bothering me because I happened to be with Carter that night in Poland. It kept bothering me, a statement that always got a big cheer.

When I got back to Washington I looked up the presidential transcript. Jimmy Carter had said absolutely no such thing at all. It's simply not true. It did not occur, did not happen, and he did not say it. A day later in a press conference on the Helsinki accords Judy Woodruff asked the question, Mr. Carter, do you think your concept of human rights is preserved in Poland?

And now I don't know whether this was the speech writer, the issues man or whatever, but it seemed to me rather interesting as an exercise in what we are talking about. Is it an issue, is it worthwhile, was it a slip, a mistake, does it say something about his campaign, does it say something about him? I don't know the answers to it. It's the kind of thing that's very hard for the press; these things are being said and you're stopping, stopping, stopping, to look exactly at the simple process of what did the man say and was he correct. If he wasn't correct, was that an honest mistake, a slip?

MR. MINOW: Isn't that President Carter's obligation, since he was there and remembers what he said, to call it to your attention?

MR. JOHNSON: That's free game tomorrow.

MR. DOYLE: That's not much more important than what happened in 1976 with the debate—in my opinion at least, lots of people disagree. Jerry Ford said something to the effect that Poland was a free nation. That was a slip. I don't think it tells us a whole lot about Jerry Ford. It tells us that in a specific debating situation he made a gaffe that a quicker mind might not have made. But it doesn't tell us his policy is bad or that on foreign policy he's inadequate. It tells us something. It's somewhat important, but that became a big issue. Bob Teeter makes the point—he was polling for Ford at the time—that in the first several hours of polling Ford was doing terrific. By the time of the morning news, radio news, etc., Ford had lost the debate—quote, lost, unquote —and the reason was because Ford shot himself in the foot when he misstated the situation. Well, I don't think that's the way we ought to frame the debate.

MR. MINOW: Speaking of framing the debate, there is one theory that Sen. Kennedy gave the speech he gave this week (at Georgetown on major energy and foreign policy issues) to get off Chappaquiddick and on to another subject because the press was only talking about Chappaquiddick. What do you gentlemen say about that?

MR. JOHNSON: He did give the television appearance on Chappaquiddick where he needs votes most, and he dealt with that question directly. How effectively, I don't know, but he did make telecasts about it.

MR. BARON: You said the press is dealing with Chappaquiddick and the press has emphasized Chappaquiddick. But the further I get away from the press the further I get away from people day to day involved in politics, and I think David Broder may have said more than anybody else did in Florida. The more discussion there is on Chappaquiddick—just walk around someplace where they are not having a primary where the candidate isn't there that day and just walk around and talk to people and ask what they think about Sen. Kennedy. When I went down to Mississippi with Reagan in September in Hattiesburg at a state college or local Baptist college, about 10 black students were standing while the luncheon was going on. I walked over and asked these students what they thought of this and that and what they thought of Sen. Kennedy. "He's the one that killed the broad," one of them said and they started to talk about that. That was the first thing that 10 black students who had not been involved—and Kennedy was not even campaigning in Mississippi—said. It's much bigger now than then, and I think it was underestimated by at least me and I don't know how many other people earlier this year. I don't think it's a creation of the press, and I don't think it's a trivial issue. I think it's a big issue and in judging the Kennedy candidacy it's an important issue.

MR. STOCKMAN: The Kennedy speech is a good illustration of something about issues in a primary setting. I don't think he was trying to enunciate any new solutions to the nation's problems. He was trying to communicate with certain activists in the party that he needs money and volunteers, that he needs to generate morale in right now. It seems to me that's what he was saying essentially—I'm not going back to the cold war, I'm getting serious about conservation and I'm going to do something tough with governmental authority about inflation, which is very different from where people perceive Carter. In the primary process, issues are ways of mobilizing resources as well as communicating with the electorate. That's what he was doing because he's got to mobilize fast if he's going to survive.

MR. BARON: The same thing Reagan did in 1976, moved on to issues, like Panama.

MR. MARLOW: I'm wondering how issues are imposed on us. Chappaquiddick is a case in point. When Sen. Kennedy came with us to do a half-hour program, the panelists who were to question him talked among ourselves before the program about whether we could do this program without bringing up Chappaquiddick. This is after the Roger Mudd CBS interview. The consensus was that, because of the error of omission, the audience is still consumed by that issue and deserved another opportunity to see the senator deal with it.

MR. JOHNSON: Are they really consumed with it, do you think?

MR. MARLOW: I gather so.

MR. MINOW: How do we know that?

MR. MARLOW: Again, as Alan Baron spoke—wherever he goes, Mississippi and elsewhere . . .

MR. BARON: I don't know that we know that. We relied on polls all summer to tell us Chappaquiddick is no longer important. We asked people, are you going to vote against him? Then we got to the point, will Chappaquiddick cost him six or eight points? Where it wasn't costing him six or eight points? We were talking of 60 or 70 or 80 percent of the people and raising the threshold of doubt about Kennedy. He might have still overcome it.

MR. MARLOW: After the CBS interview there was an issue—has he learned how to handle it?

MR. MINOW: I want to ask you a question about polls. Forgive me while I tell you a story. I was a delegate to the 1968 Democratic convention, and Illinois sat next to California. A very attractive California woman started talking to one of our Chicago regulars. She said isn't it terrible how unreliable the polls are. I said I don't know what you're talking about, lady, we can always count on the Poles. It was a half an hour before she realized we were talking about two different kinds of polls. In Chicago we talk about

P-O-L-E-S.

Why were the polls so off on Kennedy? In the summer of last year polls indicated Kennedy 80, Carter 19. What happened?

Polls and the Shaping of Opinion

MR. BARON: Peter Hart said last summer in an article in a political newsletter called the Baron Report, that the polls really were not shaped until people were forced to make a choice. He wrote, at a time when Jimmy Carter was at 19 percent in one of the polls and had no chance of winning, that he thought Carter had about an even chance to get reelected because eventually the public would focus on the issue and start to think about it and then Carter would be weighed against other men and real issues in a real decision. And I think that's very true. You go up and ask people about questions they are not concerned about and not thinking about, which was the case last summer, and Kennedy was simply a reflection of disenchantment with Jimmy Carter. Kennedy didn't lead Carter 2 to 1 a year or so ago; it was very close up until Carter's decline really started. I think it was that people weren't really focusing and never thought about Kennedy—are you for Kennedy or Carter, yes, Kennedy, that sounds good.

MR. DOYLE: The polls a year ago reduced to a snapshot that was blurry. People didn't have Kennedy on their mind or really Carter as a presidential candidate on their mind, so they voted for Kennedy, a terrific name, seems like a good fellow, he's photogenic, I see him in People magazine all the time. And Carter is the guy in the White House who everybody at the bar is always complaining about. Once Kennedy got in the race, everybody said, the polls would go down. How far depended on Carter's conduct and the world situation, and that's precisely what happened. We use the polls for more than they are, which is the news story for that day.

MR. HART: In this whole discussion and indeed the several different panels that we had, we are taking everything as of February 1 or February 2. If we had held this discussion in October, it would have been an entirely different discussion. George Bush wouldn't have had the amount of concentration and the time. We have yet to cast a single ballot for the President of the United States. We have yet to elect a single delegate and we are talking about the process as though it's all over. The process hasn't even started, and all I'm saying is the press in my estimation is going to look like a contortionist by the time this election year is over, because they are all writing that Jimmy Carter is in great shape, he's back and so on and so forth. He's not back. The fact of the matter is everything that was reported in terms of the polls in September or October and November are still there. They are right underneath the surface. It's like termites in a house: the house looks fine on the exterior, but underneath they're there.

We are talking about George Bush as though he's been nominated and will be the Republican nominee. I don't see it. The dynamics are still going to be the same, and that's what I think is important to understand. At this stage of the game, the selection process which we are going through, in which Jimmy Carter and the whole perception of how 1980 is going to play out, Jimmy Carter is seen as passive, he is seen as weak. Those perceptions are really not changed in terms of where the process is at this stage of the game.

Edward Kennedy, for example, is still seen as decisive, forceful, strong, etc. —those kinds of qualities are still there. Now, by May you'll have a whole different tenor of reporting if Edward Kennedy wins New Hampshire and he goes on and wins Illinois.

MR. DOYLE: There's a more interesting question. Supposing he loses those and then the Carter thing turns around some time late in the year, Teddy is no longer a viable "candidate" whatever happens, Jerry Brown stays in and starts winning some late primaries and Carter goes to the convention and is scarred, gets the nomination and loses the election. People are going to say the press killed Kennedy.

I don't subscribe to that. I think it's oversimplified. The fact is this whole business about being first is important, is a media phenomenon and we are now in the next couple of weeks going to decide who is still in the race because of the intensity of the coverage. The story is there, a very good story, and everyone in this room wants to read about it, but it still has the effect of blowing out the guy who does badly early.

MR. JOHNSON: We are not doing the issues nearly as well as we do who is on top of the latest poll.

MR. HART: Let me break in and say that's where the polls do "a better job." The problem is that they do a lousy job measuring the issues. When I say lousy job, I'm talking more public polls because what they are doing is distilling it down into a lot or little or yes or no or if we agree or disagree, where the issues are a lot more complex, how people come at them. What happens is we get everyone saying Carter is doing a good job or a bad job, when it's really not quite that simple. It's a broader scale and a lot more people are in the middle.

The Dynamics of the Process

MR. DOYLE: I have not seen the substantive discussion of what's happening in the Democratic Party, which is in a tremendous division when we never had a better issues campaign.

MR. JOHNSON: Isn't that our problem?

MR. DOYLE: I think it's very much our problem.

MR. STOCKMAN: On that you have a very interesting dynamic that hasn't even been reported. If you go back five weeks ago, about December 10, the

Carter Administration was moving internally in their discussions very close to something tough on gasoline conservation. They were debating whether there was going to be a rationing plan or whether it was going to be a $10 tax. Since Kennedy came out with that (proposal) Monday—in the last four or five days—you can see the stalling on the part of the bureaucrats in DOE, on the part of the spokesmen around the White House. There's been some very clear movement as an important part of the debate and dynamics of the nominating process, yet I have seen no discussion of that in the press.

MR. DOYLE: Some of the columnists made the point, but there was no general discussion. We are going to let New Hampshire be a live-or-die situation for Ted Kennedy. The concentration and focus is on that primary night audience, the people who want to know who won and who lost and get a little bit of commentary by someone about what the polling the week before showed was on peoples' minds. But we have a situation here where a candidate challenged the President and just before an important primary said, "I'm challenging him on these specific issues," and there's a clear delineation now in the Democratic Party, and the media haven't picked it up.

MR. BARON: That's in itself a commentary. You couldn't kill George Wallace in 1972 when he ran or destroy him politically, you couldn't kill him when he didn't do very well in Iowa or New Hampshire because the people who were concerned about his issues were there. Wallace didn't do well in Maryland and Michigan because those people perceived he was going to be the Democratic nominee and win in Florida. He got more publicity, but they voted for him on issues. They were probably an issue-oriented electorate. I don't think they voted for him because they liked Cornelia or he smiled well. I thought they voted for him because they thought he would reflect what they wanted. I think that was true with McCarthy and to some extent with McGovern.

I think the problem Kennedy faces is the people, the constituency that he's aiming at and that he's hearing out there, and most of the people around Kennedy haven't been out there very recently and they haven't come from out there. It's not a movement that started and came to the top. The people who started in 1972 and 1968 are up there now, but there's nothing happening out there. Rationing is an important issue, but the fact is that the liberals in Sioux City, Iowa, my home town, who organized for McCarthy and McGovern, didn't feel any moral compulsion or ideological compulsion or philosophical compulsion to rally behind Edward Kennedy. He hadn't convinced them and I don't think he has convinced them now that black Americans and poor Americans and working-class Americans on energy issues are going to be better off if he's president. Maybe it's impossible for him to convince them. The demand for his candidacy came from politicians who thought Jimmy Carter was faltering. It didn't come from people who thought if we can throw Jimmy Carter out and put Edward Kennedy in the quality of life as we see it is going to be better. That was never there. He didn't bring in new people that had never been involved in the process before and wanted to change things. I'm not sure anyone could have done that.

MR. HART: Go back to Jimmy Doyle's point, that Edward Kennedy made a definite policy alternative which is different from what the Administration is offering. There is a choice and it's before the first primary, and I think it's a vital difference on how you're going to approach the issues and what it's all about.

MR. DOYLE: That's our problem, what Alan Baron said is out there. It's a political phenomenon; we couldn't have changed that. I think the issue is not Chappaquidick, but character. It was out there, sitting out there. We may not have done a very good job of finding it. In fact, it's in the polls. It was always very hard to find, but people lately have found it in the polls—this whole business about the importance of Teddy Kennedy's character and the play-off between that and Ted Kennedy as a strong politician with strong leadership potential. It was always there to be mined. I don't think we could have done anything about the point Alan Baron made. But we can do something now about the issue-orientation of the race in the Democratic Party.

MR. MINOW: There's a question I want to put to all of you. In the first presidential campaign I ever worked on in 1952, I worked for Adlai Stevenson, who had two thoughts: One, that a political campaign was an educational experience for the electorate and for the candidate; and second, there were worse things that could happen to a candidate than losing as election. Are those two thoughts so obsolete, so horribly old-fashioned, that none of you see a campaign any more as a chance regardless of who wins to air the issues, debate them, form public opinion?

MR. JOHNSON: No, I don't think so. I think, much as the voters are more sophisticated, much more mature today, press coverage is actually better.

Bob Donovan and I were talking about this earlier, about when he covered the Truman campaign. It may have been that the coverage on issues in that campaign was better. I think we spend more time cutting away from campaigns, talking to voters, using the techniques of polling, doing long pieces on trying to find out about the background of the people—and not just the Washington Post and the New York Times. The trouble is the process has gotten out of hand. People do get weary of it; there are too many primaries. I think that we get on these planes and are trapped racing back and forth. It's very hard to be heard in that context. I don't think it's entirely our fault. I don't know how the rest of you feel, but I think there's more sophisticated reporting today—or an attempt at it. It's not good enough.

MR. MARLOW: Maybe the only decent judgment you can make about this campaign thus far is that it's been dominated by events, not issues. I'm not sure there's much you can do about that. What happened to Jimmy Carter in Iowa was dictated much more by what happened in Iran and Afghanistan. To a certain extent the same is true with George Bush. People perceive George Bush by what he says, by the way he behaves, by his background and experience as being a man who might be better able to handle that than Ronald Reagan. Those events dominated thus far. There's a long way to go and maybe we will get to issues. I don't think we can make decent judgments about how we in the media are covering the issues.

MR. HART: You don't really think anyone has formed an opinion on George Bush? A poll done on the January 9 through 13 by CBS and the New York Times says 81 percent have no favorable impressions on him, 91 percent have no unfavorable impression. Yet in the course of 24 hours he went from six percent in the polls among Republicans to 27 percent. That's got to be a creation that comes out of you (press) people.

MR. STOCKMAN: I think that tells you something about Ronald Reagan, not about George Bush.

MR. HART: Why not George Bush?

MR. STOCKMAN: It says he was a kind of parking place for Republicans.

MR. BARON: People in Iowa know something about George Bush. Nobody knew anything about the nominees 50 years ago when they were chosen by 3,000 people at a convention, and Mr. Harding was very unknown to the public before he was the nominee. The fact is a hundred thousand Republicans in Iowa know something about George Bush.

MR. MARLOW: And made a decision about him.

MR. BARON: Yes. The good thing is that 30,000, whatever it is, Republicans voted for George Bush and said, we want this guy to be considered. The good thing about the process is that the Republican Party has at least a couple of more months in which case the media has the responsibility to look at George Bush and to test him. That process is not a bad process; it's a pretty good process. We keep saying over and over again—it's become a truism—America takes too long to elect its President; let's shorten it up. If we had a parliamentary system we might be watching the leader of the opposition party for five or 10 years.

MR. JOHNSON: Don't you think it's too long? Each time it's longer and longer and longer.

MR. BARON: I'm not sure it is.

Understanding the Issues

MR. DOYLE: What's wrong is the guys who cover the political candidates who are out there for so long covering "American politics." That's what's wrong with it; it is a structural problem which gets those generalists who didn't want to become economic reporters or science editors and had an interest in politics when other people were alienated. I think the coverage is far better than it was in the Stevenson years. I was a cub reporter on the Worcester Telegram in 1956, and the political reporter then was one of many who used to hype the crowd figures for Eisenhower and lower them for Stevenson. The standards now are better and young people coming into the business are terrific. I think the people we have covering the campaigns this year are far better than they were four years or eight years ago. That doesn't mean there isn't a whole lot further to go. I think they think the coverage is boring. I think they are bored. And one reason is we do not take not take the moments of delineation when a Kennedy stands up and says, okay, he stands for that, I stand for this, and make a little bit of drama out of it.

MR. MINOW: I want to go back and be more specific about the issues. You're going to vote, David Stockman, on an energy bill very shortly. If you hadn't spent seven nights and seven days a week over the last couple years, do you think you would have any understanding what you were voting on?

MR. STOCKMAN: Yes, I think you have an understanding of the basic proposition. You might not understand the details. I have been studying it three or four years, and I can't remember quite what the tax rate is on new oil, but I think it's too high.

MR. MINOW: When you go home to your district, can you explain it to your voters so they can understand it?

MR. STOCKMAN: Yes, you can, because again I think you communicate in a kind of shorthand that tells people where you stand. And that's why I have this great trouble with the League of Women Voters' notion of campaign as an education process. Every year they send me a questionnaire with 20 issues on it and they want 750 words my position on each issue. I don't think there are more than three people who read it. But when I go out in my district and I say the government caused inflation because they are running the printing presses too fast, some people believe that and they vote for me and others don't. Now, I could give a great discussion of M-1, M-2, M-3, M-1A and B (money supplies) and all kinds of complexities. It's not relevant to the campaign trail, and it's not necessary to do an adequate job of conveying where you stand on the issues. So I really have a hard time with the view that issues are handled very badly in campaigns because of the press, because candidates are manipulative or because somehow the whole process is deficient. I think they are handled fairly well.

MR. JOHNSON: This year's is the hardest and certainly one of the most important elections I ever covered. There was a remarkable article by George Kennan in the New York Times which I think is the kind of thing that deserves wider circulation. It lays out very carefully and calmly and quietly the war and peace issue which is the first time, Kennan says, since 1945 that an atmosphere of war has been created in Washington. Looking at it very carefully, he has thoughts about it.

I have a feeling that if we get on this process, this is going to be debated in ways that will be quite serious. That is tied in with everything else—oil, energy, inflation, character. Therefore, our problem is not to lose the thread of what we have to do. If you are a reporter, you can't take too many of these weeks on the road with the candidates. It's innervating, that's our problem, and we have to find ways to solve this. The issues will be debated this year. It's a matter of survival.

MR. MARLOW: I would hope that we would see debates of the issues. I hope we will be able to see on television the candidates discussing the issues even if we in television fail to cover the issues adequately. Bill Small said at one of the earlier sessions that getting rid of Section 315 would be part of it; then the network would be able to provide special programming so that the candidates could discuss these issues. I think that would be helpful. I'd like to see networks make the same commitment for that kind of programming that they made live for Studio 8H, with Zubin Mehta and New York Philharmonic. They're saying, don't ask us how many people watched it, it's significant, it's important. I hope they do the same thing in political debates and discussion. Should that happen, then we will get some illumination of the issues.

MR. BARON: I would agree. We need a lot more time on television, a lot more coverage, more network programs like the McNeil-Lehrer Washington Week, that style of program in which there's more discussion and analysis, long programs. I think we get more of that in the printed press.

The other point that Haynes Johnson started to make is very important: That is, the people who cover politics shouldn't be traveling around with political candidates. It's fine to do once in a while. The crowds, people that go hear political candidates, are not necessarily a cross-section of the public or even the political leadership in a community. In many cases it's a star appeal. We saw the crowds Reagan and Kennedy drew in Iowa, which were phenomenal. But the people who cover politics should go beyond that and think about issues, think about longer-range electoral trends and how people are responding as related to the past. They should go out and talk to other people and spend time. Somebody should be spending an awful lot of time with people who worked with George Bush in the United Nations and the people who were with him in Houston.

You can't go by words. You have to talk with people and travel and get away from traveling with the candidate.

MR. DOYLE: James Reston said long ago that the press's opportunity and obligation, when they have peoples' attention, is to use it to educate them. In the coming year the thing that will bring peoples' attention, the exciting part of the year, is the horse race, as we call it. I hope to see a greater integration of the war and peace issues, the survival issues, whether they are economic or strategic, with the horse race, this year. Frankly it's easier for the news magazines, and if they don't do it, shame on them. Television needs to find a way to do this and needs to do it every night. Newspapers always try to do it and I think television has to find ways to do it.

MR. HART: We are basically in an era where people go for confrontation politics. We have to find ways in which—whether it be the Roger Mudd type of interview or some other way—the voter is allowed direct insight on the candidate. That becomes terribly important. One other thing in the voter's behalf: We are constantly interviewing voters from state to state, and the thing that impresses me is that they have a real impression on the issues and they have an idea and an understanding.

I mean it is not as though they are *tabula rosa* and have no opinions. They may not know M-1, M-2, M-3, but they know where they want to go and can provide some sort of fascinating insight.

Summing Up

MR. MINOW: I'm one of the few people here who has actually run and been elected a delegate a number of times. In my particular district one-third of the people are Republicans, one-third are Democrats and one-third are independents. The gripe you get from the independents is that they don't want to vote in the Republican primary, don't want to vote in the Democratic primary, and they're the guys who are going to decide the election in the fall and you're giving them two turkeys to choose from in the fall election.

Those people it seemed to me are more concerned about issues than people who will vote a party label, and it seems to me that the press has a responsibility which is so far-reaching that I hope every night as you go to sleep you stop to think about it because you are the interpreters for each of us in trying to reach a decision.

ROUNDTABLE FIVE

Reform and Counter-Reform

MODERATOR

Stephen H. Hess is a syndicated columnist and a senior fellow in governmental studies at the Brookings Institution. He has served as U.S. alternate representative to the United Nations General Assembly and as a consultant to the White House on financing cultural institutions. He also was a principal speech writer for President Dwight D. Eisenhower and later served under Richard M. Nixon as deputy assistant to the President for urban affairs. Mr. Hess is the author of seven books, including "Organizing the Presidency," "The Presidential Campaign" and "America's Political Dynasties: From Adams to Kennedy." He also has written for numerous anthologies and magazines and is a frequent contributor to the Los Angeles Times, the New York Times and other newspapers.

PANELISTS

Kenneth A. Bode is a network correspondent for NBC News.

David A. Keene is the political director for former U.N. Ambassador George Bush, and in 1976 was the Southern campaign coordinator for former California Gov. Ronald Reagan.

Martin F. Nolan is the Washington bureau chief of the Boston Globe.

Carl. R. Wagner is the director of field operations of the Kennedy for President Committee.

James Wooten is a national political correspondence and producer for ABC News.

ROUNDTABLE FIVE

How Well the System Works—Some Rankings; Some Problems With "Reform"; The Proliferation of Primaries; Advantages of the System; Resources and Strategy; Reporting on the Campaign Trail; How the Issues Affect the Process; Keeping the System Open; Choosing a Vice President; The Purpose of Conventions; Some Parting Shots; Summing Up.

How Well the System Works – Some Rankings

STEPHEN HESS: There are other ways we could choose a chief executive for our national government. Some have said in frustration there must be a better way. A long time ago we used to choose presidential nominees by congressional caucus. Some other democracies have their leaders picked by a meeting of the equivalent of our national committees. Many have proposed that candidates should be selected by a national direct primary or through a system of regional primaries. Instead, there has evolved either by design or by accident or by both our present system. It now involves 37 primaries with other states and territories choosing their delegates to the national conventions through caucuses, with these caucuses often being held in the precinct, county, congressional district and state levels.

In order to judge whether this long and tortuous way that we have devised to nominate a president needs reform, needs counter-reform, first we should get some notion of how well each of you thinks the system is working. I ask you to keep two measurements in mind. One, are the candidates who get nominated the most likely to be good presidents? And second, does the system adequately test for the qualities needed in a president?

You're all familiar with the usual scales of 1 to 10. To get the parameters of whether we are talking about drastic major overhauls or fine tuning, let's go around the table once quickly and see if we can get a number.

MARTIN F. NOLAN: Well, it's an imperfect world. I give it a 4.

CARL R. WAGNER: I gave Mr. Nolan my proxy by way of number. (Laughter) I want to add two things. I think there's a presumption that the nominating process, particularly reform and counter-reform of it, grows from conclusions reached by managers and their candidates. I think that either history or surely the future will not be dictated by that. The construction of the nominating process within the Democratic Party basically has grown out of a sense of injustice felt by constituencies, either political constituencies or demographic constituencies within the party. Whether that's proportional representation or affirmative action or winner-take-all systems in primaries, it is my conviction that counter-reform, if it occurs, will grow from the same sort of sense of injustice that parts of the electorate feel regarding the nominating process long after the candidates who have been part of it have left the scene.

In 1976 and 1977 and 1978, the Democratic Party, with the Winograd Commission, deliberated at some length over the rules and procedures before it, of choosing a candidate, and a long time was spent on the question of whether or not the nominating system should be limited to 13 weeks. And it was decided that it should be, and very shortly thereafter exceptions were made for two very notable states, New Hampshire and Iowa.

But quite aside from whether or not the party would limit primaries to 13 weeks, there's nothing to limit Florida or South Carolina or Massachusetts from conducting a straw poll in October or November or December. The extension of the calendar beyond 13 weeks is in part a function of what the party will do internally by way of managing its delegate selection system.

MR. HESS: We will get back to the specifics that you're giving, but just so we can set the parameters, so we see what we are talking about, I ask you for a number.

MR. WAGNER: Five.

MR. HESS: Okay. Ken Bode, what have we got from you?

KENNETH A. BODE: I have problems with campaign spending reform, which is certainly part of the nominating system. I think it amounts to a vast overreaction to the abuse found in Watergate. Apart from those, I would give it a seven. We have too many primaries now. I'd like to figure out something to do about that if we could. We have vastly fewer shenanigans within the nominating process now that there are rules in every state; people know when the caucuses are going to be held. The primaries we do have are better primaries than we used to have. They are more reflective of the public will. The reforms in the Democratic Party which have spilled over into the whole process and influence the Republican nominating process as well, have been basically a moderate response to some serious problems and have headed off a lot of worse ideas, like a national primary. I'd say exempting the spending reforms, a seven for the rest of it.

MR. HESS: Ken Bode gives it a seven with reservations. Dave Keene?

DAVID A. KEENE: I could have said the same thing. I associate myself with every word that Ken said.

MR. HESS: Seven on the same scale. Jim Wooten?

JAMES WOOTEN: What Ken Bode pointed out strikes me as perhaps one of the most important facets of this process, that the over-response in terms of finance takes the glitter and gleam off of some of the other reforms, but I'd give it a six or a seven.

MR. HESS: Okay. You give it a grade that would pass an undergraduate but probably fail a graduate student at Harvard. Let's see how the American people compare on that. The L.A. Times did a poll and asked the same question. Forty-three percent said that our system of nominating a president is essentially good; 27 percent said it needs some improvement; 11 percent said it needs many improvements; 16 percent want a fundamental overhaul, 3 percent didn't know. So you're about in line. But let's now see if we can get some specifics, some consensus on what is wrong, why this isn't a perfect 10 system.

Marty Nolan, you took off six points. What are the one, two, or three things that seem to bother you much on these scales of producing a person who would be a good president?

Some Problems With 'Reform'

MR. NOLAN: I have a real problem with the fraudulent word that leads our panel, reform. In the last 10 years there's been exactly one written memo to the members of the Boston Globe Washington bureau. That was an advice, admonition, indeed, a command, an order on pain of losing a finger to put quotation marks around the word reform. It's the most loaded word in the political vocabulary. I think one man's reform is another man's loophole. Any time people talk about reform, I try to put my hand on my wallet because most reforms end up corrupting themselves.

The zenith of party responsiveness and commitment and indeed the first big primaries in which people really participated in the great American democracy came about in the election of 1920, which gave us a choice between James M. Cox and Warren Gamaliel Harding, both of whom must have been pure and spotless men because both came from the newspaper business. Didn't turn out that way.

After that we had the corrupt Practices Act, Teapot Dome, and as Teddy White told us at dinner the 1968 election was probably the zenith of television's interest in participation, and the television campaign of Richard Nixon that year was flawless and so was the campaign. It really worked. There was not much in the way of technical detail you could quarrel with. John Erlichmann delivered the luggage on time and became chief of domestic programs in the White House. The reforms that followed that after Watergate produced the current system in which everyone complains about too much emphasis on these early primaries.

Somebody ought to say a good word about New Hampshire. It's very difficult to do. (Laughter) Really disagreeable little state, you know. (Laughter) No sales tax, no income tax, people flee there because they really don't like government very much. But, there are a lot of really disagreeable people in this country. They deserve representation. It's a federal Republic, a sovereign state. They could do what they want. The system is as it is. I don't think there's any ingenous national primary idea that's going to come through. So a high 4.

MR. HESS: Carl Wagner, why don't you continue with your exchanges and problems. You gave it a five.

MR. WAGNER: I think it's very hard. We have lumped together campaign delegate selection and campaign finance, and I would like to disassociate them because I think the most radical change in the selection of the president over the last 20 years, and I do think it's radical, is the campaign finance law. The resources that make it available to challengers versus incumbents, to challengers and non-incumbents the reappropriation of resources available to a campaign is staggering, especially given the inflation in the cost of campaigning. I mean it has been estimated that in 1960 President Kennedy spent in his primary races $750,000. That probably represents less than a third of the sum of money spent this year in the state of Iowa, the first caucus state, by all the candidates. Simultaneously, the ability of candidates to raise money, the constraints put on challengers and incumbents, plus the enormous reporting costs. The Kennedy for President Committee probably will spend between one and two million dollars in complying with the law. Financing in a very dramatic and noticeable way has influenced the nominating process far beyond the length of the primary season or proportional representation in Congress.

MR. HESS: You, too, Ken Bode, have some problems with campaign financing.

MR. BODE: Very simply I think all the laundered money in 1972 caused vast overreaction. I think the spending limit, for example, of a thousand dollars, is unnecessary. The most important single ingredient to the whole campaign finance process is simply reporting. If a candidate wants to take $2 million from somebody and the American public knows about it, that's all that's essential. All this business of spending limits state by state, matching funds, so forth, I think a whole lot of it really can be just thrown out.

MR. KEENE: It's silly and it's unnecessary. It screwed up the system, made it difficult for challengers and even difficult for incumbents in some ways. It was ill-considered in 1974. Former Sen. Pastore in looking back on it a year later said the members of the Senate didn't act like senators, they acted like scared rats.

There was a perceived need for reform, and the goo-goo brigade from Common Cause leaped into the breach with this proposal which has made life miserable for everybody involved in politics, has reduced discussion, has reduced public involvement and has proven once again the only thing you can count on is the reformers will accomplish almost the opposite of what they set out to accomplish.

The 1971 act, which was passed and had some problems that were taken care of by the courts, provided for full disclosure. That act was never tested because Watergate raised the question that was met with the perceived need for reform. But if the Congress was motivated by public policy concerns at this point, I think it would strike everything right back to 1971 to provide for full and complete disclosure and let the system function freely. That won't happen.

MR. HESS: But the law was passed because it turned out in 1972 that there was considerable corruption in the system.

MR. KEENE: The corruption that existed was illegal at the time it took place and it was found out at the time it took place. Nothing in the new law has done anything to make that less likely.

Take the theory behind the new reforms. It was felt by the Congress and it was felt by the reformers that the mere act of someone contributing more than a thousand dollars was per se corrupting both to the contributor and to the candidate. There's no evidence that's the fact. When the Supreme Court considered it even in upholding that portion of the act—which I personally consider a direct affront to the First Amendment—the court allowed that there was no evidence and that the people supporting the law could produce no evidence, but that there was an impression abroad in the land, and that therefore the First Amendment had to take a back seat to legislation that would cure the impression, not the reality.

If you accepted the validity of the contribution limits, then I ask, what purpose did this spending limit serve except to limit discussion and debate? In 1972 George McGovern spent something like $45 million in the general election and couldn't get his message through. Today no candidate can spend that much. That hypes the advantage available to the incumbent, the guy going in ahead.

MR. WOOTEN: Wait a minute. How is it that you reckon that George McGovern's message did not get through?

MR. KEENE: His people didn't think so, and I think they had a right to spend as much money as they wanted to try to get it through, that's my point.

MR. WOOTEN: I don't argue with that. I don't think anybody at this table would argue that the American people didn't understand what sort of candidate George McGovern was.

MR. KEENE: The point being, in those days you had the ability to go out and raise the money and to spend it, and that money is spent on communication. What's happened since then as a result of the spending limits and the law has been that campaign managers and candidates, particularly as you approach the general election, have reduced those aspects of the campaign that are not controllable and cost-effective. It's reduced anything essentially other than media campaign because that's controllable and they feel as things get moving you can utilize that.

Grass-roots campaigning dried up both for technical reasons and because you don't want to spend money on it. Any kind of outreach programs for most candidates are gone because that's not the most effective way to spend your dollars. You have put constraints on campaigns that are very, very serious.

MR. WOOTEN: Talking about the system's value in producing the best men for the presidency, the best nominees, does it prevent good men from becoming the nominee of the party?

MR. NOLAN: It may prevent competent men. The thing that worries me about this law is that it makes politics into another bureaucracy, which is pretty bad. The Federal Election Commission has already done for politics what the Interstate Commerce Commission has done for transportation, which is to bury it in red tape, to strangle it and immobilize it.

And the worst spinoff of it is what it's done to our business—the press, media, television. It's encouraged the attitude of pecksniffery that comes upon the press whenever it wins a couple of battles. Every cityroom in America is crawling with young guys in trench coats who have seen the movie too many times. They think that every politician is crooked, and by God, we are going to find out. In national politics I don't think there's any doubt that the quote, quote, quote, reform following Watergate has changed the way people look at potential presidents. People are talking about goodness or, this year compassion. These ethereal qualities.

MR. HESS: Wasn't there another underlying concern when the law was passed, the American people seemed to think that there was too much money being spent?

MR. NOLAN: Yes, money.

MR. WAGNER: I think not.

MR. NOLAN: They are wrong in that. Let's be clear on this. There were statutes on the books in the District of Columbia against burglary. They were statutes against conspiracy, subornation of perjury, and all the President's men went to jail for it. We had statutes on the book against people of evil intent. But they figured it must have been Clement Stone's money that made them that way. I don't think so. I think they would have been that way on a budget. (Laughter)

MR. HESS: We have consensus, it appears, on one point, that campaign financing reforms have gone too far, that they have driven money out of the system, money being the way that candidates translate their message to the people through the media, and that the main thing is that we know where the money is coming from.

The Proliferation of Primaries

MR. KEENE: That problem has been made worse by the proliferation of the primaries, which took place at exactly the same time they were cutting off the money supply. So that the total dollars available to any candidate was reduced at a time when the need for dollars was increased because of the way the system was changed. As we are seeing again this year, this has made momentum so very important because the money just isn't there for primaries. Candidates try in many places to ride through on whatever hype they get elsewhere. So you can argue that some of those primaries, just because of their number and the unavailability of resources to candidates in terms of time and money, are in many ways less representative than the old caucuses because nobody can participate and it just happens automatically.

MR. HESS: Even putting the question of money aside, is that another concern of this panel, that we now have too many primaries? It's gone up every fourth year, it's almost doubled in 20 years or so. The first roundtable on New Hampshire seemed to conclude that the primary plus caucus, this mixed system, was a very nice one. Is the mix wrong now? And if it is, how does this relate to getting the best people to run and to win?

MR. BODE: The mix is a little out of kilter. I'm not sure it's not going to get back in kilter, however, because one of the myths is that the McGovern rules caused all this proliferation of primaries. I really do think that's a bum rap for the McGovern commission, the original commission, because the commission distinguished not at all between primaries and caucuses. It said both of them can be democratic systems if they follow certain procedures.

Then there was a proliferation of primaries, just as there was during the progressive period when people were very unhappy with the results and the process back in 1912 and 1916 and 1920 and so forth; we had a lot of primaries.

MR. HESS: Wasn't it a lot easier for a state party to follow the rules under a primary system than a caucus system?

MR. BODE: Not likely, not at all.

MR. WAGNER: The most complicated filing system in the country, in the Democratic Party, is in Pennsylvania.

MR. BODE: Followed closely by Ohio or Illinois.

MR. WAGNER: Before the Iowa caucuses, you have to identify all your delegate candidates, all alternate candidates; in each county you had to get a notary public to notarize each petition slate.

MR. HESS: There's nothing in the rules of the Democratic Party that would really prevent us from going back or a state repealing a primary.

MR. BODE: Some states have done it. New Mexico in 1972 decided they ought to have a primary because California was getting all the attention, so they put on a primary. All party leaders in the state were behind Hubert Humphrey that year. Nobody came to the state to campaign because of California right next door. George Wallace and George McGovern split the delegation, state party leaders stayed home from the convention and the next year they went back to a caucus system.

MR. KEENE: And the Republican Party in Arkansas has done the same thing.

MR. NOLAN: Voters themselves are pretty good at reform. In the Iowa caucuses, the biggest story that struck me was not the number and identity of the candidates, but the number and identity of the voters. They took a caucus and made it into a primary—perhaps to the chagrin of Kennedy and other losers out there. They said, we don't care if it's supposed to be for just the buffs of politics, we are going out to vote, and they did in huge numbers, on the Republican side as well.

MR. KEENE: Was that a better system when it works?

MR. NOLAN: The better system is the system that gets more voters active, I don't care what they call it.

MR. KEENE: One of the things that has changed over the years is the role the primaries play. Back in 1960 you didn't have very many primaries, and candidates weren't really going into them to win delegates. They were going into them to prove they were viable candidates, that they could beat the other guys in the primaries. And they took those results to Pennsylvania and those places and argued to party leaders and people in conventions that this was something worth looking at.

So the primaries were there to demonstrate something. Today the great bulk of the delegates to either convention are selected and actually are bound in primaries, which removes a lot of the flexibility of the delegate once he is selected and also changes the whole nature of what the national convention is by the time you get there.

Advantages of the System

MR. HESS: Do we learn more about the candidates in order to make a wiser decision through the primary or the caucus system? Does the candidate learn more about the nature of the country that he may govern through one system or another?

MR. KEENE: I think one of the advantages of the primary system and caucus system, as opposed to either regional or national things, is that we force candidates to go to different states and to see the variety of different concerns and special interests in this country, which they would not see under any other system. They may not like it, they may not like to have to go to Iowa and address their concerns. It would be a lot easier to play with total wholesale politics, large numbers of people shifted through media and all that.

I don't know how much the people learn about the candidates, but it's conceivable that it's an educational process that any candidate goes through. It may teach him something about the people and about the country that he might not otherwise learn.

MR. HESS: Carl Wagner, you're in the same business with a candidate out around the country. Are they learning anything about the people, anything that's going to be useful to them if they are in the White House, or are they just being exhausted and worn down?

MR. WAGNER: I don't know. There are two things I would observe about it. One, the primary calendar extends beyond the delegate selection count. Dave Keene can speak with some certainty based on Maine, the state Republican convention straw vote there, a number of stories written in October and November of 1979 and the Florida state straw vote. The Democratic Party, I'm sure, outdistanced the analysis done on the vote with the amount of money spent by the President, trying to win the vote. The estimate was around $500,000 spent trying to win the Florida straw vote in October of 1979. Regardless of what the parties do by way of windows on which date caucuses might occur, the fact is the system has been not so much spread out more than was previously the case, but it's been pushed earlier and earlier, and it's being pushed earlier and earlier not by the parties so much as by to some extent the media and to some extent by challengers always looking for a narrow shot.

MR. HESS: But the media pushed this process, extended it, made it long. Haynes Johnson doesn't like that, but you fellows are on the road with candidates. Does doing this long process gives you more time to really figure out what makes this candidate tick and to tell your consumers whether this candidate would be a good president? Or would you, too, rather have a much shorter opportunity?

MR. BODE: I would say that the process is not too long. We are a federal republic, and there are 50 states doing it in 50 ways and taking some time to do it. It's a useful thing for Sen. John Kennedy to encounter the kind of people he encountered in West Virginia, or for Jimmy Carter to encounter the people he did in Iowa, or for George Bush to see those people and for them to evaluate him. I don't think it's too long a process.

Nor do I think we ought to continue with the party reform and make it a perpetual process. Most of the reforms have been codified; they are in state parties' rules all over the country. There is a general agreement about those reforms, and how we should get on with it. One thing, and that is these phony contests, straw polls: It's within the preserve of both national political parties to tell their state parties, no more straw polls. A bunch of baloney. It's draining on the candidates' time, a drain on treasury. It's a hoax. We should have no more. And the media shouldn't have covered it the way we did.

MR. WOOTEN: One of the things we are talking about here is simply a degree of difficulty. People do become president through this process, as difficult as it is, as expensive as it is, and as restrictive as the campaign financing laws are. It can be done, to wit, James Earl Carter. The fact that it is more difficult for campaign managers, strategists and technicians to handle doesn't seem to me to really address itself to whether it is good or bad. We can make value judgments on President Carter or on Gov. Reagan. But the fact of the matter is that it is possible to weave your way through all of this and to become the nominee and then the president.

MR. HESS: Jim Wooten, you followed Carter in 1976, knew him as well as any member of the press, wrote a book about him. Do you conclude that after he went through this process he was in better shape to govern the country, he knew things that he didn't know before?

MR. WOOTEN: Yes. I think Carter found out some things about the country and about himself. I'm not sure that they stayed with him. (Laughter)

Resources and Strategy

MR. HESS: It has been said, though, that under this system that now starts so early and goes on and on, that in order to succeed, you have to be unemployed. Jimmy Carter was unemployed in 1976. George Bush is, and that gives him a pretty good chance to spend his days on the trail. Is there anything to that, that this long system discriminates against the worker, the fellow who is in the Senate?

MR. KEENE: Yes and no. You analyze a candidate's resources when you're working with him and the candidate should do it himself as well. In 1980, on the Republican side the various candidates have different resources. And to the extent that one campaign applied those resources in the way that they should have and others didn't take advantage of all of those available to them, the candidate's time is only one. It's a valuable resource but not the only resource available. It's conceivable, for example, that some of the other candidates using a different mix of resources could have come out much better. And it's easy to say that if a candidate finishes here, then you look at what he is and say these are the peculiar characteristics of candidates that make it necessary that it end that way. It isn't that way. That may only have been a coincidence, or it may be that, lacking some of the other things, that candidate did things that he had to do and others might not have had to do. And without going into the specifics of what the other candidates were doing, the fact is that there is a strategy and a tactic that can be developed for all the viable candidates. They use a different mix of resources and they can be used effectively.

It's not really reasonable after it's over to say that the guy who did it had the mix that was the only one that would have worked. Another mix might have worked and somebody else might have won.

It's like, now you talk about the candidates have to use the Carter strategy. Well, if somebody else had won, it would have been their strategy. If it had happened in a different way it would have been given a different label and we would all have been doing something else. That happened to work at a specific time and under specific circumstances with resources applied by a specific candidate. That doesn't mean it's the only way.

MR. WAGNER: You can't overstate that. There's a presumption, first of all, that the system works the same way all the time, that the rules are applied with the same sort of constraints or advantages in a race where everyone is a challenger. It works the same way there as it does in the race where you have an incumbent and a challenger. The difference is in the dynamics of the Republican Party in 1980 with six or seven challengers versus 1976 with an incumbent and a challenger. The advantages or disadvantages of Gerald Ford or whoever versus Ronald Reagan, if he's the front-runner now, are staggering, mainly because you have not factored into consideration the ability to manage the debate. Ultimately the political decisions are made, elections are won and lost, as this one will be in 1980, on the ability of a party or candidate to speak to the issues the country is concerned with, and the management of that debate is the central objective of a campaign.

MR. BODE: It seems to me it has quickly become the new conventional wisdom that the only way you can run for office is to be out of a job, and therefore the system really does't test the great qualities we need for a president. Jimmy Carter didn't win the last time just because he *didn't* have a job —and Mo Udall didn't lose it just because he *had* a job.

The old system still existed in 1968. I wonder if we all remember how Richard Nixon got the nomination, and what he did throughout 1966 and 1967 to pay his dues around the country to get that nomination; how much time he spent. Or go back to the really good old days in 1960. When John Kennedy got the nomination, he spent the entire year of 1959 going around. He was wooing party leaders, admittedly, with John Bailey at his side. He had to go around to caucuses and early primary states. I have no doubt that John Kennedy would have spent equally little time in the Senate (under the current system).

Reporting on the Campaign Trail

MR. HESS: Let me ask the press here, how does this long system affect you in your coverage? One of the previous panelists was very concerned about the cynicism he saw in reporters. How do you keep your perspective, day after day, month after month, being locked up on that bus?

MR. BODE: Families suffer.

MR. HESS: What does this mean to media coverage? You're telling people that you get too close to the candidates. Marty Nolan once wrote a marvelous piece called "Faust at the Race Track." Are you all in there on inside dopester stuff after you're stuck together for so long? And what can be done about it?

MR. NOLAN: If we are supposed to be reporters, we entered this business with half-baked romantic notions of what we are supposed to be. If we still stick with them, I guess we still stick with the business. If we are to be the herald and tribune of all good virtues, we are concerned whether it's a fair fight, for instance, and that keeps you going and keeps your equilibrium.

So if you hear this argument where you have to be out of a job to run, I think of Sen. Baker, who thought he would parlay his great TV exposure, when he was Dr. Watson to Sam Ervin, and be presiding over the defeat of the SALT treaty that he would do single-handedly on television. Well, things didn't work out that way. Sen. Kennedy was way ahead in the Democratic polls last summer because he represented a fantasy—aspirations and hopes of peoples' nostalgia dreams—and then reality came. Nobody expected Jimmy Carter to do his imitation of God and Franklin Roosevelt and Douglas MacArthur. (Laughter)

So life is unfair. That was why I only gave the system a four. The wonderful thing about the newspaper is that it comes out every day. So you really can't hold onto your crazy theories very long because you're very often wrong. I have been wrong on practically everything in 1979, but you have a chance to come back. I don't think cynicism is a problem. If it were, I think we would be out doing public relations for button factories.

MR. BODE: What grows out of the question you asked about reporters being locked up with candidates in the mother ship as they travel around, and you set your baggage outside the motel room door and somebody picks it up for you, has a Bloody Mary ready for you: the only newspapers you read are the newspapers on the seat of the airplane, because that's all that's available to you. That is a big problem and I think that every newspaper and television network that has correspondents locked up individually with candidates for long periods of time ought to rotate those people from one candiate to the other so their perspective doesn't get dulled and their wits dimmed by the whole process.

I feel myself, when it happens, getting dumber by the day as we travel from stop to stop. I don't think I understand the candidate particularly better the third or fourth or fifth day for having been along that long. I think that's a problem.

MR. WOOTEN: I disagree. I don't think there's anything wrong with rotating correspondents from candidate to candidate. The problem is what is expected of a correspondent who is assigned to a candidate. If it is expected of him by his newspaper or his network that he cover the campaign from inside that cigar tube, that's wrong.

In 1976, from my own experience of being locked up with one man for nearly 13 months, I don't think that objectivity or fairness waned, or that cynicism increased at all. I think that kind of exposure and sort of constant assignment contributed to a better overall report.

MR. NOLAN: Can I give the best illustration of this? Because it comes from a distinguished alumnus of this great institution, Henry Adams. Henry Adams graduated from Harvard in the 1850s and decided he didn't have anything better to do, that he would go into the newspaper business. And he wrote dispatches for newspapers in Boston and wrote about Sen. Sumner, the great liberator of the day and very powerful orator who had been a friend of the Adams family. He wrote something about Sen. Sumner that Sumner didn't like, Sumner being a very vain man. And in Lafayette Square near the White House young Adams was walking along and said hello to Sen. Sumner. Sumner looked through him. Later, in "The Education of Henry Adams," Adams wrote, "It was then I discovered a principle, as sure a principle as arsenic poison, that a friend in power is a friend lost."

That's the first thing we know about the newspaper business—some stiff gets elected to city council and he thinks he's God Almighty, or we get too close to him and we confuse it. As long as we know a friend in power is a friend lost, we'll be alright.

How the Issues Affect the Process

MR. HESS: There's one other thing that came out and was controversial in an earlier session, and that was how this process deals with the real issues. Bob Scheer of the L. A. Times certainly felt the candidates didn't. Jimmy Doyle of Newsweek didn't think that the media was doing a very good job covering the issues. On the other hand, Peter Hart and Congressman Dave Stockman seemed to be saying to us that the basic issues somehow emerged in about the degree of generalized discussion that met the needs of the average voter.

We have been criticizing the system, occasionally praising it. Why haven't we said anything yet about how candidates and media are dealing with issues?

MR. WOOTEN: The system as we have it provides the opportunity for whatever issues are germane, whatever issues come from the reality of the campaign to be aired. The problems are quite finite. In terms of getting issues before the voter, before the electorate, the problems are ours and the candidates. In 1976, Carter managed to give the perception of an issue-oriented candidate while avoiding any real substantive position-taking on most of the issues. He gave the perception of being a man who was quite willing to discuss the issues with you, when in reality he discussed no issues at all in that campaign—and did it as cleverly and as skillfully as I have ever seen done.

MR. KEENE: Maybe we should be backing up and coming to this. I'd like to say something in defense of, if not campaign managers, at least of the people who actually make the choices in the primaries and the caucuses. The cynicism that comes out sometimes in the press, and the campaign managers and the candidates, is because a lot of the discussion internally is how do you do this to get these people and how do you do that to get the others. But my impression has always been that the voters are a lot smarter than any of us give them credit for.

Coming at it from an ideological perspective, I might like to say the way we should select our candidates is that they should all present their positions on 19 issues and then we ought to judge them. Some of that goes on and a lot of issues get discussed, a lot of people see that.

But we don't know, none of us, really what it is that the people out there are going to make their decision on. It's a mix. They are trying to make a prospective decision about these candidates, and when we talk about who is a good candidate or who will make a good president or who is right on the issues, that's something we are saying coming from our viewpoint. It goes in whenever you hear a discussion of how things are being covered. How the hell do we know all of what the people out there want to know about the candidates and about the issues and about that mix?

The voter is perceptive enough and smart enough to know that what he really has to do is choose somebody who not only has positions that he likes, but who is going to have to deal with problems that can't be perceived at the time the selection is made. It's when this whole mix comes together that none of us knows how to gauge, none of us really knows what in the final analysis makes one candidate click in that way when another one doesn't. Part of it is the issues, part of it is something else, part of it is something very vague. And to try to catalogue it and to say, "This is good and that's bad and we ought to do more of this," that's all fine. But the real cataloguing and the real decisions are made out there by voters and they do a pretty good job of it.

MR. HESS: If the voters are as smart as you say, is that the reason that the participation level keeps dropping? Shouldn't we be worried about that?

MR. KEENE: It should be noted first of all that the participation level in large measure has dropped because of the expansion of the electorate and that a major component of the decrease in voting participation has taken place as a result of expanding the electorate to the young, for example, who don't participate in as great numbers as other groups in the society.

Beyond that—this is maybe an ideological observation to an extent, but I don't think so—there are people who might not participate because of the judgment on their part that they don't make any difference, that participation in voting doesn't really affect their lives. That's a growing perception. I refuse to believe that in all instances it's an irrational perception. It may not be a perception that we like, it may not be a perception that is good for the system, but in some cases it's rational. Large areas of the impact that government has on people have been removed from control by elected officials and by the people. And it's their perception that candidates don't make any difference that's led to this proliferation of referenda, the Proposition 13 thing in California and all that, where voters are saying, by God, none of these guys make any difference and if we are going to have anything we are going to have to do it ourselves. Now, we might not like that, but I think that's another symptom of this whole thing and I'm not certain that's entirely irrational on the part of the voters.

MR. HESS: Ken Bode is shaking his head either yes or no.

MR. BODE: If you look at the polls—post-Watergate and post-Vietnam polls—you see a slump of confidence in this country, in the system, at least the component parts of the system. How is the President doing? Lousy. How is Congress doing? Worse. Is there any difference between the two parties? None that I can tell. So it's no surprise that voters who hold those attitudes about the actors don't participate much in the process. At one point pollsters began to pick up in 1976 in the primaries a positive intent among people not to vote. "No, I'm not going to vote. I won't have any part in the process, I don't want to be blamed for the outcome, I don't want to have any part in the outcome."

I think that's rather a dangerous kind of phenomenon to have. I don't think it's anything permanent. It's the kind of thing that will bottom out as people begin to perceive that the process works, produces decent people and decent government. It will be okay. Why shouldn't people be cynical about Watergate and Vietnam?

MR. KEENE: It may have bottomed out and be moving upward. Participation in the Iowa caucuses is unprecedented, and it's one of the questions we face as we approach the other contests: is that reflective of something outside Iowa? Is there some sort of disquiet out there that's going to result in tremendous turnouts that we can't right now predict in the primaries?

Keeping the System Open

MR. HESS: Will anyone speak up for moving to a national direct primary? Any enthusiasm on this panel?

MR. KEENE: It's a crazy idea.

MR. BODE: No.

MR. HESS: Down, all voted down. The Gallup Poll of January 20 said 66 percent of the American people favored a national primary, 24 percent opposed it and 10 percent had no opinion.

MR. KEENE: Those are the same people who are also happy with what is done now.

MR. HESS: How about the regional primary system? Anybody like to speak up?

MR. BODE: One of the things this process has to have is a measure of accountability in both parties. It's got to be possible to challenge the leadership and stewardship of the incumbent President.

In 1968 it was really clear that, in the Democratic Party at least, a lot of people didn't like Lyndon Johnson's policy on the war. They wanted a test of his stewardship and they didn't get it through the nominating process, which set off all these reforms. Now we have a real test of Carter, or would have if the Ayatollah hadn't intervened.

Any time you have a single simultaneous test in six or eight or 10 places at one time, you advantage the guy who is the front-runner, the incumbent. Insurgents, challengers have got to have time to raise money slowly, build momentum slowly, have a few tests in Iowa and New Hampshire and move across the country. That's very important if you're going to have any accountability in a nominating system and it's vital in this democracy. I think a regional primary is a bad idea, and those people who want it really want it because they want things simpler. Give them a little time and they will sort things out for themselves. They'd figure out the system we have now.

MR. NOLAN: Democracy is supposed to be messy. Nobody says it's supposed to be neat and packaged. There are significant differences between people in Oregon, people in California, and certainly the people in Massachusetts and New Hampshire. You ought to celebrate those and welcome them instead of trying to squeeze the toothpaste back into the tube. What's the point of regional primaries? I never understood it.

MR. HESS: Let's move on to one matter that hasn't been discussed at this conference yet. It is part of the presidential process, and that's the selection of a vice president. Is there anybody who would argue that, as it is now, it's an afterthought of a tired, exhausted group of delegates hand-picked by the nominee and that there should be a better way to do that? Last week two Republican state chairmen asked for a change in the way their party did it. They proposed that each contender for the presidency submit in a sealed envelope a list of three to five people who would be acceptable to the candidate as vice president, should that candidate be nominated.

MR. WAGNER: Bad idea.

MR. KEENE: Promising things to poor turkeys.

MR. BODE: John Sears had a good idea in 1976: Announce before the convention who your vice presidential choice would be so you have a ticket there. If delegates don't like it, they can say so. It's not a bad idea.

MR. HESS: Then they would have to reject their candidate for president by rejecting his nominee.

MR. KEENE: The way it's set up now is the vice presidential selection is the first real decision that the nominee makes—and it says a lot about the nominee. Ken Bode is saying that, if you want to reform it, let's not take that decision away from the nominee. Let's let him make it at another time. I don't think you want to just throw that open.

MR. HESS: What about what the Democrats stumbled into quite by accident in 1972 when they had to change vice presidential candidates? Some weeks later they reconvened. They then had had time to think it through. The candiate had had time to assess the different possibilities, apparently something he had given little thought to the first time around, and they chose another nominee.

MR. KEENE: The fact is, that first decision was not an illogical decision. It was a rational choice and the thing that made it a bad decision was not something that they necessarily would have discovered another way.

MR. NOLAN: What we witnessed thereafter was George McGovern going around the country getting the door slammed in his face.

MR. WAGNER: If the system produced over recent history the evidence for change, you would interrupt the change, the one remaining thing candidates have at their disposal, take that away from them? Vice presidents that have been produced have been adequate, have done a good job.

MR WOOTEN: I always liked Spiro Agnew.

MR. HESS: Anybody remember Charles Bryan, Henry G. Davis?

MR. KEENE: You wouldn't have remembered them if they were selected another way.

MR. NOLAN: Probably the only time the founding fathers took their foot off the bag was in creating the vice presidency. It's a totally useless office. Look at all the people it's ruined. Hubert Humphrey, Richard Nixon (Laughter), sitting there waiting and checking Ike's pulse every time he shakes hands. (Laughter)

Exactly 50 years ago this fall the Shubert Theater in Boston gave a tryout to this wonderful musical comedy, "Of Thee I Sing." Alexander P. Throttlebottom says it all, "Every vice president is a Throttlebottom." As Thomas Riley Marshall said: He is a man in a catatonic state. He cannot speak, but he hears everything that goes around.

MR. HESS: Thomas Marshal also said what this country needs is a good five-cent cigar. There is some wisdom in the office. Can we at least agree on the one little proposal put forth by an Institute of Politics Harvard task force a couple of years ago that we could change the order of business at the convention, put the platform between the nomination of a president and vice president and thus give a presidential nominee an extra day to think about it? Is that too much to ask?

MR. BODE: Sure:

MR. WAGNER: Fine.

MR. HESS: We shoe-horned one reform in. (Laughter)

MR. WOOTEN: If you look at what Carter did in 1976, between the time when it became clear that he would be the nominee and the convention, one might argue with his choices, but he dealt very seriously with the subject and it was so demeaning. He paraded all these people down the red dust streets of Plains.

The Purpose of Conventions

MR. NOLAN: I would like to abolish the national conventions—how is that? (Laughter) They have not served a useful purpose since 1952. There has not been a second ballot since 1952. Since 1952 they have done nothing but ratify the choice of the voters in the primaries. That's all they will do this time. There's not going to be any deadlock at these conventions that we are going to spend all this money and time going to. They could do it by mail. Conventions are overdone and overblown.

MR. BODE: That's too radical. If it really is a problem that they just ratify the choice, all we've got to do is backtrack, counter-reform, change a rule that Roosevelt changed and go back to the two-thirds rule. You would get a better party consensus behind a candidate, you would have a much more interesting convention, no question about that.

MR. HESS: David Keene, speak for the conventions.

MR. KEENE: They haven't been much since 1952, with the increase in binding primaries taking the independent judgment away from the delegates. But the fact is that something can happen between June 3 and the time the delegates meet in convention. There are judgments, and I think that the convention is important not just from the standpoint of platform—whether or not anybody reads it afterward—but it does tell you something about the party, something about where the candidate might supposedly want to go if he's listening to his party. We have done too much in this country to diminish the role of the party generally as an institution. It played a valuable role in the past. Parties have been much maligned; we have moved into a candidate-oriented kind of politics, which I don't think is healthy. We ought to think about ways of strengthening the role of the party and perhaps strengthening the role within the nominating system of that convention as opposed to diminishing it even further or abolishing it.

I don't particularly enjoy conventions either, but I think they are necessary and I think they potentially provide something valuable to the system that we should strengthen, rather than get rid of.

Some Parting Shots

MR. HESS: Each one of you deserves one final crack at last thoughts having to do with whether this system is working.

MR. NOLAN: Beware of the word reform, with or without quotation marks. Particularly beware of it when it's accompanied by a six-point program with four sub-proposals for every point. Particularly beware of it if it comes out of a great academic institution. And remember that the vote for president is the least ideological decision any American ever makes. They vote for a man of character, and they don't vote for a problem solver as much as a decision maker. So anything that enhances the public's approach and visibility of the candidate's character is something that ought to be encouraged. If there's a hundred primaries, it's all right with me.

MR. WAGNER: As to the objection of the system as extenuated or too long, the challenge that is posed is far, far less than you suggested in the current conversation. The challenge to campaigns and to the press in covering campaigns is to really address the issues before the parties, and I think there's agreement that there are parties in an ideological sense. Voters perceive it, and the election system as we have constructed it is centered not on substantive differences between individuals, it's centered on candidates and the logistics of candidates and the movements of candidates.

As to Jim Wooten's point earlier when he talked about the plane and the press, the point of the press being with the candidate is to cover the candidate, not to cover the campaign or the premise of the campaign.

Voters see it to some extent as a parade of individuals and not a serious debate of a decade or, for that matter, of four years. It's the toughest problem I think our campaign faces, given the constraints of the system and the finance law.

MR. BODE: Happily, I'm not as suspicious of reform as Marty Nolan is, with good reason. But I think that at the moment we have tinkered with the process almost enough. Each year demonstrates to us a little bit of what's right and what's wrong about it, and for the most part things are basically right now except for the campaign spending laws, which require a serious reevaluation, and the problem that Carl Wagner raises, which is that the process has been artifically extended back into the previous year with the straw polls and so forth.

By and large, I think we are almost through an era of reform that began with the apportionment decisions and produced the 18-year-old vote, campaign spending reform, party reform and so forth. It's not been a bad era altogether. It think it's almost over, and we're ready to let the process work itself out.

MR. KEENE: I started by agreeing with Ken Bode and I'll end by agreeing with him.

MR. WOOTEN: I think this system is as imperfect as the politicians who plan it and use it and the candidates who live or die by it and the press that covers it. It occurs to me that the role of the press in the system that has evolved has become even more important, and that the whole idea of equity ought to be in the minds of the press in terms of covering this kind of system. It's quite easy for the system to become inequitable—not through rules, but through the abuse of loopholes. The press has to be perhaps hypercautious and hypersensitive to the inequities that are potentially in this system.

Summing Up

MR. HESS: We started a while back by voting on the system. We didn't give it very high marks; they ranged from 4 to 7. But then as we started to look at the alternatives, we were suspicious of reforms. We couldn't quite figure out a better way, although we did suggest a series of fine-tunings. We worried particularly about campaign financing, the present spending limitations—I think we feel most strongly about that.

There are other things that worried some of us, if not all of us—certainly the question of straw votes and artificially expanding the election beyond the election year.

And so we conclude perhaps where one of your colleagues in the press, James Flansberg of the Des Moines Register, did. Most of us were out there in Iowa last Jan. 21, and if we picked up the Register on the 22nd, we would have read a long article by Flansberg. He concluded by saying this, and he's a little more optimistic than you gentlemen:

"A strong case can be made that we have accidentally stumbled into a good system and don't yet realize it.

"One telling point is the self-cleansing effect. If a candidate goes to New Hampshire and tells how he is going to cut the cost of home heating oil, he's eventually going to have to go South to explain whether he proposes to do that by making the Sun Belt help subsidize Northern heating costs. He's going to have to go to Texas, Oklahoma, Louisiana and account for how he's going to cut their gas and oil prices."

There are "dozens of examples," he says. "If you want to talk about cheaper food costs in the urban East, you must be prepared to explain why you promise the folk in Iowa and downstate Illinois and Wisconsin and the rest of the Farm Belt higher prices for their beef and their grain and vice versa.

"Beyond that, the present system adapts itself to the candidates.

"The system teaches Ted Kennedy and Jimmy Carter something about corn and hogs, or at least the politics of corn and hogs. It teaches Jimmy Carter about the cold places where heating oil costs nearly a dollar a gallon, or at least the politics of such places. And it teaches Ted Kennedy something about peanut farming and how it is a social welfare program in disguise, or at least the political manifestations of it.

"It's a marvelous system because it teaches the politicians who presume to guide us that we are crazy, beautiful, political quiltwork. Any major change in the system jeopardizes that teaching facility. The reformers are ignoring a natural law: When something works, don't fix it."

AFTERWORD

AFTERWORD

By JONATHAN MOORE

Looking back at the conference in early Febrary and ahead to the publication of this book, it is easy to conclude as a general proposition that the Los Angeles Times and the Institute of Politics had a good idea and—with the help of some very able and interesting people—carried it off well. The sponsorship joined the resources of a newspaper and an academic institution, the subject-matter bridged political process and media coverage, the participants combined working political and journalistic professionals. In addition to the direct experience of the audiences at the sessions in the Public Affairs Forum at the Kennedy School of Government and of those in more private and informal corridor conversations and exchanges at meals, the national poll conducted by The Times, the public television specials on each of the five roundtables, and this book promise to provide a good overall distribution of the product.

But beyond all of that, how helpful was this ambitious and spirited enterprise in increasing understanding of the nominating process and the media coverage of it and in developing ideas for better coverage? How far did we penetrate the subject matter so that new insights were gained and new solutions discovered? Was any consensus developed out of the diversity of experience and interests represented?

The answers to these questions are more elusive and ambiguous. No wholly new breakthroughs were achieved, but some juicy pieces of meat were chewed—new insights revealed, motivations bared, and analytical connections made. We proved better at defining existing problems and criticizing pending solutions than discovering or constructing new ones, respectively. There was a lot of differing opinion, although interestingly not so much along occupational cleavages, and some intriguing consensus.

Although the between-Iowa-and-New Hampshire scheduling reaped special benefits, holding the meeting so early in the season denied consideration of this year's electoral experience after we had learned a great deal more about it. As Walter Mears of Associated Press said, "It's a little early to see what the election of 1980 is about because it hasn't taken shape yet." In an important sense, we were talking more about 1976 than 1980; if we had been meeting in November, 1980, the conversations and conclusions would be very different. It was acknowledged that the shakedown of the new nominating procedures and campaign finance laws was still going on, that everyone should keep an eye on the abuses that had been spotted, and that it was too early to pass judgment on a system just being tested.

As for the participants, their vocational and operational responsibilities limited as well as enhanced the value of their contribution. The highly developed expertise and active roles of the participants made it difficult for them to get the distance and detachment to enable them in turn to address fully the questions put to them and be creative about change. Indeed, they have an interest in the existing system not being changed in ways that might diminish their influence, and this may to an extent explain a general level of satisfaction with the system as it works now, or at least an uncertainty as to how to improve it. To a limited extent, the moderators played the role of detached critics, but they had enough to do to guide the participants through the assigned subject matter. In panels where the participants did make a successful effort to draw back to evaluate and question their own roles, the product of the discussion was more valuable.

One bright idea the designers of the conference had which fell somewhat short was to identify the "linkages" between process and coverage—that is, to define instances when the structure of the nominating system directly influenced the press coverage or vice-versa. Either this was too ambitious or there aren't many causal connections, but a few were found. One which was developed involved the relationship between media habits and the proliferation of state primaries. Several participants believed that the benefits to be reaped from media attention were an important incentive for states that changed from a caucus-convention system to a primary election. The more primaries proliferated, James Naughton of the Philadelphia Inquirer further pointed out, the more the media would tend to concentrate on the "horserace" aspects of campaigns: " . . . who's up, who's down, who's rising. We are increasing attention to the mechanics of the system rather than to the substance." This effect, it was pointed out later, can then in the same cycle lead some states to revert from primaries back to caucuses (for instance, Arkansas and New Mexico; maybe Nevada and North Carolina), on the grounds that the desired media attention failed to materialize. They discovered that coverage depends more on the given state coming early in the process than to the delegate selection model used.

Another example of the symbiotic relationship between the process and the press that was discussed at several points during the conference involved the proliferation of more costly state primaries at the same time a money squeeze was being put on campaigns by the new finance law's expenditure limits. The financial crunch has the effect of making candidates much more dependent on the media. By shifting the role of carrying the candidate's message from the candidate himself to the news media, as Rick Stearns of the Edward Kennedy campaign observed, "we made the news media the most powerful actor in the nominating process."

Curiously, the final roundtable on reform largely overlooked coverage as distinct from process improvements. Throughout the conference, journalists tended to identify the problems or abuses in press coverage as arising from the system itself. They tended to admit that media behavior amplified emphasis on personality over issues—on drama, blunders, the volatility of the voters, the "filtering" function that judges momentum and picks winners, and so forth. But they insisted that they hadn't invented the system and shouldn't be held responsible for its procedural defects. This leaves the question of what interests and incentives do the media have to try to counter such weaknesses. Aside from who or what caused the problems, can the press do anything to improve the situation, to help make campaigns more serious and substantial?

Even though few prescriptions were offered on this point, concern and commitment were articulated frequently. Republican political consultant Clifton White spoke with frustration about "the horserace aspect of our campaign, the amount of time and money that the media spends trying to figure out who is going to win . . . that is just fantastic today." And political newsletter publisher Alan Baron argued that "the people who cover politics should go beyond that and think about issues, think about long-term electoral trends and how people are responding as related to the past." But there seemed to be consensus as well among the media participants that they had an obligation to try harder to place immediate events in a larger context and with a broader perspective. James Doyle of Newsweek said, "The whole business about being first is a media phenomenon . . . The story is there, a very good story . . . but it still has the effect of blowing out the guy who does bad early." And Bob Scheer of the Los Angeles Times argued, "The issue is not whether you abandon the system, but whether we adopt a more self-critical attitude of our work and whether we try to do our jobs in a better way."

The bottom line, of course, is how well the overall system works. When asked in the last session about this, the panelists came up with a 5.9 out of 10 rating. Individual answers to more specific questions throughout the conference were similarly negative or ambiguous. Does the system reward values which make a person a good President? "Maybe, maybe not." Does the system prevent good men from becoming the nominee of the party? "It may prevent incompetent men." Are candidates learning anything about the people, or just getting exhausted? "I don't know." Jim Wooten of ABC News observed: "I think this system is as imperfect as the politicians who plan it and use it and the candidates who live or die by it and the press that covers it."

The dialogue never got to the more fundamental and troublesome question of whether the system provides enough incentives to attract people to try to become President as distinct from selecting among the ones who haven't been discouraged or alienated from giving it a run. This invisible factor is hard to measure, as was implied during discussion of a speech by author Theodore White, who had identified the three permanent issues in American life as "bread and butter, war and peace, black and white," and was looking for what the 1980 election was all about. Anthony Day of the Los Angeles Times suggested that it might be "a collapse in leadership, a collapse in presidential aspirants," and White answered, "I wish I could say to you that I saw that guy on the horizon right now but I'm walking around looking for him."

There was comment both in and out of the roundtables about cynicism, and there was evidence of it in the exchanges between hard-bitten, campaign-tested political reporters and operatives; for instance, concerning mutual "conning" about candidate's expectations, and the motivations behind certain political strategems. But there were the vital life signs of idealism, also; for instance, in concern for the fairness of the process in not favoring the incumbent over the challengers, and in the respect expressed for the voters' attitudes and choice. There was a lot of self-examination and role evaluation on the part of virtually everyone at the conference. When it broke up, the people faced with the day-by-day task of managing and reporting on the nominating process may have gone away more reflective about their roles and responsibilities. In any event they had shared their thoughts with many others.

APPENDIX: LOS ANGELES TIMES POLLS

LOS ANGELES TIMES POLL
January 27, 1980

By GEORGE SKELTON
Times Assistant Metropolitan Editor

Professors, pundits and politicians often complain that America's system of nominating its presidential candidates is too drawn out, too awkward, too exhausting, too costly and unfair. But the voters like it just fine.

They like the primaries, the polls, the debates, the national conventions and even using their tax money to help finance campaigns.

They like the press coverage of the current race, but are a bit tired of stories about Chappaquiddick.

They like the political system, but not the politicians especially.

They think the voters in primary elections should have more influence over who become the nominees, and feel that contributors, political leaders and special interest groups now have too much.

They admit to learning little during the primaries about a candidate's leadership qualities, administrative abilities, solutions to problems and trustworthiness.

When pressed, nearly half do not even know whether their state holds a primary—as opposed to a series of caucuses or a state convention—to choose delegates to the national conventions.

Still, four in 10 say they are "very much" interested in the present campaign and half would like to get more news about it. (Only one in 10 want less.)

And "taking everything into consideration," eight in 10 say the nation has a "good" way of "choosing the people who are going to run for President."

The Los Angeles Times Poll interviewed 1,047 adults, including 766 registered voters, on Dec. 16-18 in an effort to measure the attitude of Americans toward the primaries, the politicians, the parties, the press and the political system generally.

For the most part, their attitude is upbeat.

In his, "The Making of the President, 1960," author Theodore H. White praised the primary as "America's most original contribution to the art of democracy." There were 16 presidential primaries when White wrote that 20 years ago. They have more than doubled in number since then, to 37 this year.

The opportunities for direct citizen participation in the presidential nominating process clearly are on the increase, due largely to political "reforms" initiated in the late '60s. In 1968, for example, only about 40% of the national convention delegates were chosen in primaries. This year, about 75% will be.

The voters obviously welcome the trend.

Those surveyed were asked whether they are satisfied or dissatisfied with these elements of the American political process: political parties, debates between candidates, public financing of campaigns, national nominating conventions, opinion polls and primaries.

Rating particularly high were primaries, polls, conventions and debates. People were more divided over parties. The results, among all adults:

	Satisfied	Dis-satisfied	No Opinion		Satisfied	Dis-satisfied	No Opinion
Primaries	79%	18%	3%	Debates	60%	35%	5%
Polls	66%	28%	6%	Financing	54%	40%	6%
Conventions	60%	34%	6%	Parties	53%	46%	1%

Democrats were more enthusiastic than were Republicans about polls, debates and the parties.

A higher proportion of Democrats than Republicans also felt that, overall, "the way we go about choosing the people who are going to run for president" is a "good" one.

When measured against America's "system of business and industry," the presidential nominating process rated virtually as high. It was more highly regarded than the political system generally and far surpassed in esteem the nation's "system of administering justice."

The result:

	Basically Sound	Not Too Sound	Unsure
Business, Industry	71%	23%	6%
Nominating Process	70%	27%	3%
Political System	62%	35%	3%
Judicial System	49%	48%	3%

The political system was particularly favored by people with at least some college education and those whose families earn more than $25,000 annually.

The citizens' relatively low regard for the judicial system contrasted, somewhat ironically, with their more positive attitude toward judges generally. And while the political system received high marks, the politicians decidedly did not.

Those surveyed were asked, "Which one or two of the following kinds of people do you respect the most: policemen, public officeholders, newsmen, judges, businessmen, ministers or union leaders?" Ministers and policemen were by far the most respected. The least were union leaders and officeholders.

The result: (adds to more than 100%)

Ministers	53%	Newsmen	18%
Policemen	41%	Officeholders	7%
Judges	23%	Union leaders	5%
Businessmen	18%	Don't know	5%

Roughly three-fourths of those surveyed said they are able to learn only "a little" during the campaigns about whether the candidates can be trusted, whether "they are able to run the country effectively" and "how they will solve the important problems of the country."

The "personal qualities" people said were missing the most in politicians who run for president were "honesty" and "leadership."

Those interviewed were read a list of personal qualities and asked which "one or two" they generally considered to be missing in the presidential candidates "these days."

The answers: (adds to more than 100%)

Honesty	48%	Faith in God	18%
Leadership	35%	Convictions	13%
Experience	22%	Compassion	8%
Competence	21%	Don't know	7%

But a majority nevertheless felt that primary voters should have more influence over who is nominated. Those interviewed said these elements, in order, should have less influence: campaign contributors, "party leaders and officeholders," "organized groups with strong beliefs," "people who aren't registered in the party," and "the press."

Of those surveyed, 74% said they "regularly follow news about politics and government by reading newspapers." This was particularly true of college-educated and higher income people.

An even larger number, 85%, said they regularly watch television news. This was especially true of Democrats.

The most interesting running news story for those surveyed was the Iran hostage situation, with 92% saying they were following it "closely." After that came "energy and gas shortages," 86%; "which prices are going up and down," 78%; "relations between Israel and the Arab countries," 52%; "the 1980 presidential campaign," 51% (another 41% were following it "casually"); "what happened to Sen. Kennedy at Chappaquiddick," 29% (especially among Republicans); the SALT II treaty, 16%, and the stock market, 15%. (The survey was taken before the Soviet invasion of Afghanistan and President Carter's consequent shelving temporarily of the SALT II treaty.)

Slightly more than half those surveyed desiied more news about the presidential campaign; only one in 10 wanted less news about Chappaquiddick, with only roughly one-fourth wanting more. People particularly asked for more news about energy and prices.

The press generally received high marks for its coverage of these stories, ranging from 2 to 1 ("good" over "poor") for Chappaquiddick to 11 to 1 for Iran. Both in its coverage of the current campaign and its overall reporting "of the way candidates are chosen," the press received 8½ to 1 approval.

The coverage of Sen. Edward M. Kennedy (D-Mass.) was the most controversial of any of the candidates, with only 42% believing it was "fair," 30%—particularly Republicans—saying the press made him "look better" than he really is, and 23% contending it made him "look worse."

By contrast, 63%—particularly Republicans—said GOP front-runner Ronald Reagan received fair coverage, with 17% believing he was made to "look better" and 12% "worse" than he really is.

The only candidates thought to "look worse" in the press than they really are were President Carter and former CIA Director George Bush. Carter was believed to be treated fairly by 59% of those surveyed, but Bush by only 46%.

Other candidates considered by a majority of those interviewed to be treated "fairly" were Sen. Howard H. Baker Jr. (R-Tenn.), John B. Connally and Gov. Jerry Brown.

The survey was taken specially for a conference—titled "Nominating a president: The process and the press"—to be sponsored by The Times and the Institute of Politics of the John F. Kennedy School of Government at Harvard University, Feb. 1-3.

The telephone interviews were supervised by The Times marketing research department under the direction of Times Poll Director I. A. Lewis. The margin of error for this size sample is considered to be 4% in either direction.

PUBLIC OPINION AND THE NOMINATING PROCESS

By WILLIAM SCHNEIDER and I.A. LEWIS

In recent years, the process by which Americans select their party nominees has come under considerable scrutiny. Both political parties, especially the Democratic Party beginning with the McGovern Commission, have undertaken extensive studies of the mechanism and have implemented their findings in reforms which will affect the nomination of the next President. Nor has the subject been neglected by academia, with notable contributions from Austin Ranney, Christopher Arterton and others. Indeed, this roundtable discussion is yet another example of a widespread interest shared by the worlds of politics and education.

Yet very little has been heard on the subject from Americans themselves who are, after all, its main actors and in whose service the nominating process has been devised. In the hope of adding this important voice to such discussions, the Los Angeles Times Poll last December conducted a nationwide telephone survey of 1,047 adults, 769 of whom are registered voters, containing a variety of questions dealing with the selection system and the role played by the press in the nominating process.

The principal findings are unequivocal: Americans are highly satisfied with the way they choose presidential nominees. In fact, the nominating system is regarded more highly even than the political system as a whole and more people, as the following table shows, consider it "essentially good" than they do our capitalistic system of business and industry.

	Is basically sound		Is not too sound and needs	
	And Essentially Good	But Needs Improvement	Many Improvements	Fundamental Overhaul
System of nominating a President	43	27	11	16
System of business and industry	30	40	15	8
Political system	17	45	19	16
System of administering justice	13	36	26	22

To this somewhat surprising popular distinction between primaries per se and the entire political system can be added another dimension: a separate attitude toward the people who operate within the process. These three viewpoints sort themselves into fairly well-defined levels of approval:

79% are satisfied with primaries;

70% think the nominating system is basically sound;

62% think the political system is basically sound;

53% are satisfied with political parties;

10% think party leaders and officeholders should have more influence than they do now,

and only 7% respect public officeholders.

Add to this layering of opinion the fact that only one group is regarded as not influential enough—primary voters—and a pattern may be discerned: the closer the process comes to popular democratic expression, the more satisfactory it seems, while the closer the process moves toward self-interest and entrenched bureaucracy, the less it is approved of.

How does the public differentiate between the nominating process and the political system?

Survey respondents were asked whether they were satisfied or dissatisfied with each of six aspects of the nominating process—political parties, debates between candidates, public financing of political campaigns, national conventions, polls and primaries. Favorability toward the nominating process was correlated with approval of primaries, polls, conventions and political parties (it was correlated very weakly with approval of debates and public financing). Primaries, polls, conventions and parties are, of course, an intrinsic part of the nominating process (debates and public financing are less so). Therefore, it is not surprising that support for all of them goes together. Attitudes toward the political system, however, were related to only one institution on the list—the political parties.

Thus, when people were asked to assess "the way we go about choosing the people who are going to run for President," they seem to have had in mind primaries, polls and conventions, if only because those were the previous topics of the interview. Primaries, polls and conventions are democratic and popular, and all received highly satisfactory ratings. Political parties had the lowest rating, with 46 percent expressing dissatisfaction. According to evidence from other surveys, political parties tend to be seen as narrow, self-interested and undemocratic. For example, in the 1978 national election survey taken by the Center for Political Studies at the University of Michigan, respondents were asked, "How much do you feel that having elections makes the government pay attention to what the people think—a good deal, some, or not much? A majority, 56 percent, said "a good deal." But when asked how much political parties help to make the government pay attention to what the people think, only 21 percent said "a good deal." The political system probably has stronger elitist connotations than the nominating process. When asked to assess the political system, people may think of parties, politicians and bureaucrats, as well as the Constitution. While parties are intrinsic to the nominating process as well, the process includes some important democratizing influences—primaries, polls and conventions, where "the people" have a say.

Figure A summarizes the three most important factors influencing attitudes toward the nominating process: education, support for the political system and attitudes toward political parties. Favorability toward the nominating process declines with education, while it rises with support for the political system and with approval of political parties. Conversely, critics of the nominating process are found most frequently among the well-educated and among critics of the political system and of the parties. The effect of education stands out more strongly in Figure A than in Table 1 because support for the political system is held constant. The college-educated are more favorable to the political system, and that tends to moderate their opposition to the nominating process.

TABLE 1

	Education		
	Did not finish high school	High school graduate	Attended college
Our political system is . . .			
Basically sound	58%	54%	72%
Not too sound	36	43	26
Our system of nominating a President is . . .			
Basically sound	75%	72%	66%
Not too sound	19	25	32
The way we go about choosing the people who are going to run for President is . . .			
Very or fairly good	87%	77%	77%
Very or fairly bad	10	20	22

It is not surprising that distrust of the political system and of parties produces disapproval of the nominating process. The latter is the instrumentality through which the parties influence the political system. If you don't like either the agents in control of the process or the results, then you are probably not going to like the process itself. But the impact of education is more puzzling. Why are the well educated less supportive of the way we choose our presidential candidates? Is it because they are higher in social and economic status and therefore resent the "populist" connotations of polls, primaries and conventions? Or is it because they are more aware than others of the defects of our

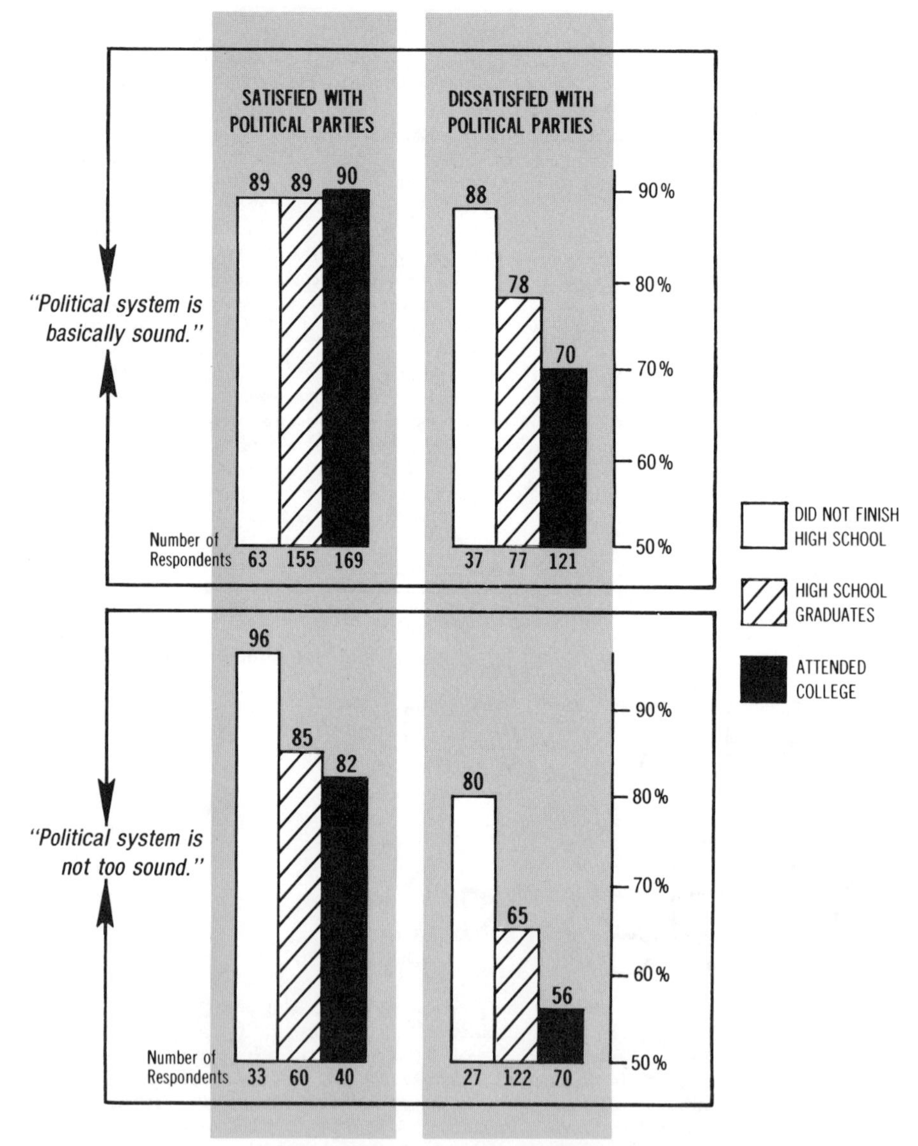
APPROVAL OF PRESIDENTIAL NOMINATING PROCESS, BY:
• Education
• Support for political system
• Satisfaction with political parties
SATISFIED WITH POLITICAL PARTIES
DISSATISFIED WITH POLITICAL PARTIES
"Political system is basically sound."
89 89 90
88 78 70
Number of Respondents 63 155 169
37 77 121
"Political system is not too sound."
96 85 82
80 65 56
Number of Respondents 33 60 40
27 122 70
90% 80% 70% 60% 50%
DID NOT FINISH HIGH SCHOOL
HIGH SCHOOL GRADUATES
ATTENDED COLLEGE
Bars show percent who rate the nominating process "Very Good" or "Fairly Good".

FIGURE A

nominating process—that it doesn't work the way it is supposed to? If so, what kinds of measures do critics feel may be necessary to improve it?

One can get some idea of what critics had in mind by looking at their answers to the series of questions on groups influencing nominations. Respondents were asked whether each of six groups should have more influence, less influence, or the same amount of influence as they do now on the choice of candidates for President: party leaders and officeholders, people who contribute money to political campaigns, primary voters, the press, "organized groups with strong beliefs," and "people who aren't registered in the party." The public felt that each of these groups, with the exception of primary voters, should have less influence. A simple index can be created by taking the percentage who said that a group should have *more* influence and subtracting from it the percentage who said that the group should have *less* influence. The most negative result was for campaign contributors; 8 percent favored more influence for this group and 61 percent favored less influence, leaving a net margin of -53. The margin for the press was only slightly negative (-11). In the case of primary voters, the net margin was positive, that is, in favor of giving them more influence in the nominating process.

Is criticism of the way we choose our candidates associated with opposition to particular influences? Table 2 compares the views of those who were favorable and unfavorable to the nominating process on the desired influence of each of the six groups named above.

TABLE 2

Desired Influence of Six Groups in the Presidential Nominating Process, by Evaluation of the Process

Figures show percent favoring "more influence" MINUS percent favoring "less influence"

	Evaluation of the nominating process:			
Desired influence of (group named) . . .	All	Good	Bad	Effect
Party leaders and officeholders	—39	—34	—61	—27
People who contribute money to political campaigns	—53	—50	—74	—24
The press	—11	— 7	—27	—20
Organized groups with strong beliefs	—36	—34	—48	—14
Primary voters	+ 44	+ 42	+ 53	+ 11
People who aren't registered in the party	—24	—30	— 2	+ 28

"Good" = respondents who rated nominating process as "very good" or "fairly good"
"Bad" = respondents who rated nominating process as "very bad" or "fairly bad"

Rank of items is based on differences between net effect of good minus bad.

Critics of the system were more likely than others to say that party leaders, campaign contributors, the press and "organized groups with strong beliefs" should have *less* influence on the choice of the candidates. Of course, even those who like the process felt that these groups should have less influence, but the point is that opposition to them was consistently higher among those who disliked the process.

Education has the same effect as criticism of the nominating process. The better educated, when compared with the less-educated, wanted party leaders, campaign contributors, the press and organized issue groups to have less influence. On the other hand, the better-educated were more favorable than the less well-educated to primary voters and to those outside the party.

What party leaders and officeholders, the press, money contributors to political campaigns, and organized groups with strong beliefs have in common is that they are all *special interests*—groups that want to influence the nominating process for their own ends. (It is interesting that the press fits this pattern, i.e., an organized group outside the process with its own interests to promote.) On the other hand, primary voters and "people who aren't registered in the party" are both *popular* groups. The arguments that primary voters are usually a small segment of the public and that independents and crossover voters may infiltrate a party's primary for mischievous purposes do not seem to carry much weight in the public's view. The fact is, anyone can register and vote in a primary, even if not many actually do so. And "people who aren't registered in the party" can mean principled independents and those who don't usually participate, as well as crossover voters. Primary voters and people not registered in the party are forces that *open up* the nominating process and make it more democratic. Party leaders, campaign contributors, the press and organized groups with strong beliefs are undemocratic influences that distort the popular will and make nominations unrepresentative.

Thus, to summarize, everyone wants party leaders, campaign contributors and organized issue groups to have less say, and everyone wants primary voters to have more. Those who are unhappy with the process want to see the press have less influence and do not feel that those outside the party should necessarily be excluded. The answer to the question posed earlier is that critics, including the well-educated, are not antipopulist in their sentiments. In fact, they are just the opposite. They are unhappy with the undemocratic aspects of the system. They feel that special interests should be curbed and the process made more open and popular.

On the other hand, well-educated people support the press more consistently than the average and, indeed, press coverage of the nominating process is regarded even more highly than the process itself.

	GOOD	BAD	NOT IMPORTANT	DON'T KNOW
Press coverage of the way candidates are chosen	85	11	2	2
The way we go about choosing the people who are going to run for President	79	19	1	1

Other stories that are considered well-handled by the press are the situation in Iran, relations between Israel and the Arabs, energy and gas shortages and inflation. Somewhat lower ratings (but still better than two-to-one approval) are registered for the SALT II treaty, Chappaquiddick and the stock market.

Generally speaking, stories that receive the closest attention by the public get better marks for coverage. There is a similar tendency to criticize the treatment of a story if the public has less interest in its subject matter.

The strongest indictment of the press concerns news coverage of Sen. Kennedy's difficulties at Chappaquiddick Island. Forty-eight percent of Americans think there should be less coverage of that incident and only about a quarter of them want more. (Even Republicans want to hear less about it.) The public also thinks that the senator is being treated less fairly by the press than are any of the other major political candidates. (The same question asked three months earlier indicated that President Carter was felt to be treated less fairly by the press than was Kennedy—but that was when Carter, not Kennedy, was the underdog.) Nevertheless, roughly half of the public believes the press is unbiased toward all the candidates tested, with the remainder fairly evenly divided between those who think the press treats them better than they deserve and those who think they are treated worse.

These findings show quite plainly that there are wide differences of opinion separating critics of the process from the voters who see no present need for reform. Indeed, there is a touch of gentle irony revealed by an educated class that insists on democracy for the people whether they like it or not.

And there is an important lesson here for the press. Many people have argued that the party reforms of recent years which appeared to be "democratic," actually enhanced the role of certain special interests. By limiting the influence of "party bosses" and "fat cat" contributors, the reforms may have increased the influence of organized pressure groups, political action committees and the press. The press will want to maintain its substantial public support by demonstrating the absence of self-interest to its critics.

But there is an overriding practical lesson, too. Any changes or reforms are likely to meet public opposition unless they are "democratic" in nature. There does not seem to be any significant popular constituency for "de-forming" the candidate selection process and increasing the role of elite groups such as party leaders and contributors. The first task for those who want to improve the system is to demonstrate to the public that it is undemocratic or manipulated.

———

This Los Angeles Times Poll is one in a series of nationwide surveys designed to measure public attitudes on a number of critical issues. The study was based on 1,047 adult men and women residing in the continental United States. Interviewing was conducted from Dec. 16 to Dec. 18, 1979.

The telephone sample was stratified according to the geographic distribution of the population and weighted to account for differences in household size. Telephone numbers were generated by computer from all listed residential telephone exchanges, and final digits randomized to ensure that listed and unlisted numbers were properly included in the sample.

Theoretically, one can say with 95 percent certainty that results based on the 1,047 respondents in the sample differ by no more than plus or minus four percentage points in either direction from what would have been obtained by interviewing every adult in the United States. Similarly, the results based on the 769 registered voters nationwide are accurate to within plus or minus five percentage points.

I. A. Lewis was the director of the survey, which was conducted under the general supervision of John Foley, assistant managing editor of the Los Angeles Times. Susan Pinkus of the Marketing Research Department of the Los Angeles Times was in charge of telephone interviewing and data processing specifications. William Schneider is The Times' political consultant.